GHOST STORIES

of MISSOURI

True Tales of Ghostly Hauntings

A.S. Mott

LONE
PINE

Lone Pine Publishing International

The Publisher: Lone Pine Publishing International
Distributed by Lone Pine Publishing
1808 B Street NW, Suite 140
Auburn, WA 98001
USA

Websites: www.lonepinepublishing.com
      www.ghostbooks.net

National Library of Canada Cataloguing in Publication Data

Mott, A. S. (Allan S.), 1975-
  Ghost stories of Missouri / A.S. Mott.

  ISBN-13: 978-976-8200-17-4
  ISBN-10: 976-8200-17-0

  1. Ghosts--Missouri. 2. Tales--Missouri. I. Title.

GR110.M77M595 2006   398.2'09778'05   C2006-901452-3

Photo Credits: Every effort has been made to accurately credit photographers. Any errors or omissions should be directed to the publisher for changes in future editions. The photographs in this book are reproduced with the kind permission of the following sources: Paul Cowan (p. 202); Lisa Fann (p. 142); Lise Gagne (p. 170); Loretta Hostettler (p. 149); Sandy Jones (p. 195); Jim Jurica (p. 132); Maciej Laska (p. 153); Jack Lamour (p. 61); Library of Congress (p. 4–5, p. 104: pan/6a07148); Rene Mansi (p. 23); Lofti Mattou (p. 26); Greg Nicholas (p. 179); Lou Oates (p. 92); Jim Parkin (p. 77); Martin Sach (p. 97); Kathy Weiser/www.LegendsofAmerica.com (p. 11, 16); Jessica Zeigler (p. 52).

The stories, folklore and legends in this book are based on the author's collection of sources including individuals whose experiences have led them to believe they have encountered phenomena of some kind or another. They are meant to entertain, and neither the publisher nor the author claims these stories represent fact.

PC: P5

To All the Gwilliams of This World

Contents

Acknowledgments

Being a writer means that sometimes it is your prerogative to annoy your editor to such a degree that no court in the land would see fit to convict them if they were to suddenly snap and stab you to death with one of their ubiquitous red pens. I am so thankful that I have been blessed to work with several editors who have had enough patience and strength of will to fight back their desires to commit justifiable homicide and allow me to live. Chief among these candidates for sainthood is Carol Woo, who edited this book in particular. I want to thank both her and the good men and women who served the coffee that soothed her during those moments when lesser mortals would have been inclined to make a go for my throat.

I also would like to thank Sheila Quinlan who helped edit the manuscript, as well as Willa Kung who took the said manuscript and transformed it into something that looks like one of those new-fangled books all of the kids are talking about these days.

And, of course, I want to thank you for picking up this book and I hope you enjoy reading it as much as I enjoyed writing it.

1
Unusual Events and Places

Lifestyles of the Rich and Infamous

There is a kind of insanity that can only be nurtured in those who have access to great wealth. It is a kind of madness that us poorer mortals will never know, as its pernicious reach extends only to those who can afford to be constantly idle and indulge in their every single desire. Around the world families with vast fortunes and influence have been brought down by this psychosis of prosperity, as their sons and daughters flout society's conventions to satisfy their basest whims.

For proof of this you have only to look at what happened to the offspring of Johann Adam Lemp, a German grocer who moved to St. Louis in 1838 and who turned his homemade beer business into a nationally recognized brewery, becoming a millionaire many times over in the process. It is a lurid tale, filled with elements that would seem ludicrous in even the most melodramatic soap opera, but it all really happened and its consequences can still be felt today. The place that was once known as the Lemp Mansion has been called one of the most haunted buildings in America, and once you hear the whole story, you'll understand why.

Johann, born and raised in the German town of Eschwege, came to St. Louis with the simple dream of earning enough money to take care of his family. He started with a small grocery store on what is now Delmar and 6th Street. It was little different from any of the other neighborhood stores that could be found throughout the city, save for its stock of a light golden-hued beer he homebrewed himself. He had learned the recipe from his father and it proved to be a local sensation. Its taste was unlike anything else being brewed in St. Louis and people traveled from the far ends of the city to get their hands on a bottle or two.

Two years passed, and in 1840 Johann closed down the grocery store and started a small brewery. Very soon it became evident that the small building could not handle both the brewery's production and storage needs, so Johann purchased a limestone cave located at the city's southern edge. With the use of ice blocks from the Mississippi River, the cave served as a perfect refrigeration unit.

With his business firmly established and his product earning prizes around the state, Johann became wealthier than he had ever thought possible when he had first come to America all those years ago. He died a happy man in 1862 and left the world not knowing that he would be the last person in his family to pass on with any kind of satisfaction or contentment.

His fortune and his business passed down into the hands of his son William. Almost immediately William set about expanding the brewery, purchasing the land above the company's limestone storage caves. By 1864 the new brewery was built and covered five city blocks, making it one of the largest such enterprises in the country. The Lemps prospered even more in the years that followed. In 1868 William's father-in-law built a beautiful mansion just a few blocks away from the brewery and William purchased it from him eight years later in 1876. After an expensive renovation that left it even more opulent than it already had been, William decided to connect the house to the brewery by building a tunnel from its basement that led to the company's limestone caves.

By 1895 the Lemp brewery had started marketing a new beer called Falstaff, named after the larger-than-life character made famous by Shakespeare. It was the first of their line of products to achieve national distribution, and its popularity transformed the company from a local institution into an American one.

But in 1901 the first of the family's many future tragedies ended their six-decade long run of good luck. Frederick Lemp, William's oldest son and future heir, died at the age of 28 owing to sudden heart failure. It was an incredibly shocking death. Always the picture of good health, there had never been a single incident in his past to suggest that his heart would betray him at such an early age. The news of it so devastated William that he never recovered from his grief. He spent three long years in seclusion, only allowing himself to be visited by family and his closest friends. Among them was another Frederick, Frederick Pabst, whose own brewery had been built with his friend's generous help. His death, which came as suddenly as William's oldest son's, proved to be the last straw for the Lemp's patriarch. On February 13, 1904, he took a pistol and shot himself in the head.

A month later the family business was officially taken over by his younger son, William, Jr. Had William, Sr., been in a more stable set of mind before he decided to take his own life, he would have likely taken steps to make sure that this did not happen, but by then he was too far gone to care.

Lemp Brewery Tower

William, Jr., was a poor substitute for his late brother. A libertine and a boor, he was married to an equally spoiled heiress named Lillian Hadlen. She was a tiny woman (some reports suggest she barely rose above four feet tall), but was considered quite beautiful for her time (though photographs from that period prove that hers was a beauty not easily captured on film). An eccentric woman with a taste for expensive things, she gained renown as the

Lavender Lady, a nickname she earned owing to her obses-
sion with that particular color. She was so dedicated to her
favorite hue that everything she owned was painted or
dyed lavender, including the horses that pulled her lavender carriage throughout the streets of St. Louis.

With the invention of modern refrigeration techniques,
the brewery no longer needed the limestone caves to store
its product. Rather than leave the caves and the tunnel
from the Lemp Mansion empty, the space was converted to
hold a theater and a large swimming pool, where William,
Jr., enjoyed throwing decadent parties that would have put
the most debauched ancient Romans to shame.

Money meant little to him. He decided to keep his wife
distracted from his numerous infidelities, by ordering her
to spend all of her free time shopping, with the caveat that
she had to spend at least $1000 a day or never be given
another penny for the rest of their marriage. This bizarre
ultimatum ensured that she was so busy trying to fill her
daily quota of purchases that she was seldom home
enough to catch him cheating on her with any woman
willing to give him the kind of attention he desired.

It was only a matter of time before he suffered some
kind of consequence for this behavior—it came when one
of his servants gave birth to his illegitimate son. Very little
is known about the bastard Lemp, but what little was
revealed is the stuff of gothic nightmares. Born with
Down's syndrome, the boy was kept a virtual prisoner in
the mansion's servants' quarters. No record of his birth
was ever made and his identity was kept such a secret that
even today no one knows his real name; he is referred to
as either the Man-Child or by the cruel and hateful

nickname, the Monkey Face Boy. It would be easy to dismiss his horrible life story as simply an unpleasant rumor were it not for the tiny plaque that sits above his grave in the mansion's backyard. Its message consists of only a single name, Lemp, and is the only monument to his existence.

After years of barely attempting to hide his bad behavior from his wife, William, Jr., finally decided to divorce Lillian in 1908, thus freeing him to be as openly wicked as he pleased. The legal proceedings quickly turned into a media circus, with all of the city's newspapers devoting full pages to describing the sordid details of the Lemps' personal lives as they were recounted in various witnesses' testimonies.

Despite ample proof of her husband's countless trysts and wild orgies, Lillian's case was nearly undone when his lawyers were able to supply the court with a photograph that showed her smoking a cigarette. Were it not for her impassioned testimony (which she delivered while wearing a black dress, and was the only time anyone saw her wear a color other than lavender) this single photograph could have cost her custody of her children in an era when women were held to a much higher moral standard than men.

During this time, William, Jr., was allowing the company his father and grandfather had so carefully built to be driven farther and farther into the ground. The rest of the city's brewers had joined together to form a company called the Independent Brewing Association, a move that forced the Lemp Brewery to contend with a level of competition it had never previously dealt with.

But since his fortune was secure even if the family business went under, William, Jr., saw no need to worry about the fate of the brewery. When Prohibition came in 1919, he felt almost relieved that the liquor ban forced him to close down the brewery for good. Thanks to his typical lack of empathy or concern for others, the men and women who had worked at the brewery for years only discovered that they were unemployed when they went in to work one morning and found the building locked.

By that time he had been remarried for four years, having tied the knot with a widow named Ellie Limberg, but this second stab at marriage did little to change his ways. In the years following the closing of the brewery, he sold many of its assets for fractions of what they were once worth. In 1920 his sister, Elsa, followed in their father's footsteps and shot herself when she became overwhelmed with marriage difficulties. Two years later, William, Jr., became the third member of his family to commit suicide. After a lifetime of self-indulgence, he could no longer find anything in life that he could take any kind of satisfaction from, so—in the same room where his father died—he shot himself with the same gun.

His brother Charles became the fourth person to carry out this brutal family tradition. Charles, an obsessive compulsive who lived in constant fear of germs, inherited the Lemp Mansion, which he renovated back into a residence from the office building his brother had turned it into in 1911. He did not live alone in the house, for his brother's illegitimate son was still alive and hidden from the world in the attic of the servants' quarters. The nameless Lemp's short, miserable life finally came to an end sometime around 1949. His half-brother, William III, had died six years before when a heart attack claimed him at the age of 43. Their uncle Charles joined them in the afterlife when, on May 10, 1949, he shot his dog—a very loyal Doberman Pinscher—and then himself. His body was found on the stairway leading up to his room.

Out of all of Johann Lemp's grandchildren, only one died of a natural cause. Edwin Lemp lived all the way to 1970, when he died at the age of 90, but even he wasn't spared from the madness that had caused so much damage throughout his family. In his will he ordered that his personal valet burn his entire art collection and all of his family artifacts, thus ensuring that certain secrets were never revealed and that no one else could take pleasure in the art he had owned. He was the last of the Lemps, having left behind no children to carry on his name.

From 1950 to 1975, the Lemp Mansion went from being a boarding house in a slightly seedy neighborhood to a nearly condemned flophouse in one of the worst parts of town. It was during this 25-year period that the first reports of the many ghosts who are believed to haunt the mansion started to leak out to the public at large.

A man named Dick Pointer had heard these stories but chose to ignore them when he purchased the building with the intention of renovating it into an opulent restaurant and inn. But it didn't take him long to discover that there was more to these stories than just a few unfounded rumors. Yes, the ghosts in the Lemp Mansion were very, very real.

As soon as the renovations began, workers began talking about strange things they had seen in the house. Some saw hazy shapes hover and float in front of them, while others reported hearing inexplicable sounds and many more complained of having their tools vanish, even when

The Monkey Face Boy often played under the eaves in the attic.

they had left them unattended for just a few seconds. Many of the workers quit, insisting that unemployment was preferable to dealing with potentially angry spirits. But enough of them stayed on to finish the renovations, and the resulting tourist attraction remains open and owned by Pointer to this day.

Although sightings of paranormal activity have occurred throughout the entire building, there are three spots where that activity has been extremely consistent over the years. The first spot is the basement, which the hotel's employees refer to as the Gates of Hell. Access to the underground caves where William, Jr., committed most of his acts of lewd debauchery has been closed off, but that has done little to keep the spirits away. The second spot is the mansion's main stairway and the third is the attic, the life-long home of William, Jr.'s, bastard son.

Though there have been few visual sightings of ghosts in the Gates of Hell, it is the place where a visitor is most likely to hear phantom sounds and be overcome with a tremendous sense of dread. More visible spirits have been seen on the mansion's stairway, but they are often unidentifiable because they lack the distinctive characteristics of the building's more famous phantoms.

Naturally the attic is haunted by the spirit who was kept a virtual prisoner inside the space for his entire life. The Monkey Face Boy's easily identifiable visage has been frequently seen peeking out onto the street from one of the attic's small windows. Visitors have reported hearing him pleading for help. Toys have been deliberately left in the room to see what would happen to them, and they have seldom been found in the spots where they had been left.

But even though these three spots remain the most reliable places in the mansion in which to have an other-worldly encounter, some of the most memorable moments in the building's ghostly history have occurred in other, less frequently haunted parts of the building.

Among these other areas is William, Sr.'s, room, where some have heard the sound of feet running up the nearby stairs before they start kicking furiously at the room's door. It is believed that this is connected to the fact that when William, Sr., shot himself, the sound of the gunfire caught the attention of William, Jr., who—upon finding the door to the room locked—proceeded to kick it down with his feet.

Also inside William, Sr.'s, room, the sound of a team of horses pulling a coach along the street in front of the mansion was heard. When the tour guide who heard the clattering hoof steps turned to look out the window to see the coach, she saw nothing but an empty street.

Though Lillian Lemp was famously cast off and divorced by her husband, it didn't stop her presence from being felt within the mansion she was so callously kicked out of. In William, Jr.'s, former room, a portrait of his ex-wife dressed in her trademark lavender clothes hangs, which would undoubtedly have been unwelcome in the room when he was alive. Visitors to this room have frequently reported smelling the scent of lavender, especially when they stand close to her portrait.

William, Jr.'s, reputation as a womanizer goes a long way toward explaining why his ghost has been most frequently spotted in the downstairs women's bathroom. Once his own private washroom, he now seems to enjoy returning to this room for the opportunities it allows him to spy on its female occupants.

One woman, a patron of the hotel restaurant's bar, was using the facility when she saw a man's face peeking over the side of the stall. She shouted at him, and he was gone by the time she was able to extricate herself from the stall to look for him. Understandably angry, she returned to the bar and saw that only three men were left at the bar, including the bartender.

"I hope you like what you saw," she said scornfully.

When the bartender asked her what she was talking about, she explained. He then informed her that neither of the two men could have been the Peeping Tom since neither one left the bar while she was gone. But this wasn't the first time the bartender had heard a woman complain that she'd been spied upon, and he knew enough to tell her that she had just earned the attention of the mansion's famous former owner.

For William, Jr., to spend his afterlife as a pathetic voyeur makes perfect sense considering his predilection for the female form and his desire to waste all of his potential in the name of satisfying his insatiable lusts. His story serves as the archetypal account of the rich boy who squandered all that he had inherited because he was simply too spoiled to appreciate it. The rest of his family fared little better.

There is a reason why our culture remains so fascinated with stories of the rich and famous, and it is not simply because they allow us to daydream scenarios in which we are as fortunate as they are. There is the burden of comfort and free time that comes with wealth, both of which are precious in small doses, but potentially lethal when they are no longer countered by the effects of worry and hard work. The ghosts of Lemp Mansion serve as a message to everyone who wishes that they could live in an opulent mansion: sometimes it is better to want than it is to have.

Into Thin Air

There are some mysteries that are so inexplicable that they defy any kind of rational explanation. When logic fails to provide any kind of natural solution to these unsolved riddles, many turn to the supernatural to find the answers that they seek.

It was June of 1968 and the Lions Club organization was holding its annual national convention in Dallas, Texas. Jerrold Potter, a Lions Club member in good standing, was joined by his wife Carrie and 19 others as their chartered DC-3 departed from Kankakee, Illinois, on its way to Dallas. The plane was being flown that evening by an experienced pilot named Miguel Cabeza.

Jerrold lived in Pontiac, Illinois, where he worked as an insurance executive. He was a very friendly, sociable man who not only belonged to the Lions Club, but also virtually every other similar organization that Pontiac had to offer. Jerrold and Carrie had raised two daughters who were now both grown and married. Freed from their parental bonds, they were suddenly able to travel as often as they could afford and they eagerly grabbed every opportunity that came their way to do so. When they learned that the Lions Club convention would be in Dallas, they wanted very much to be there.

The two of them sat quietly in their seats for an hour as the other passengers chatted quietly among themselves. Then, as the plane flew over the town of Rolla, Missouri, Jerrold was overcome by the call of nature.

"I have to go to the washroom," he whispered to his wife as he stood up.

"I'll be here when you get back," she smiled at him, before she returned to the magazine she had been reading.

Jerrold yawned and stretched his legs and started walking to the back of the plane where the lavatory was located. Along the way he saw an old acquaintance named James Schaive, president of Ottawa, Illinois, Lions Club chapter, and stopped to talk to him.

Carrie could hear James laugh and turned to see him and her husband talking, before Jerrold stood up and continued on his way to the washroom. She went back to reading her magazine and waited for him to return.

He never did.

*   *   *

Back in the cockpit, Miguel Cabeza and his copilot, Roy Bacus, were in the middle of what had—up to that point—been a textbook flight. Everything changed when Miguel noticed that one of the lights that shouldn't be flashing, was. "DOOR OPEN," informed a bright red light.

"Damn it," cursed Miguel when he saw it.

"What's wrong?" asked Roy.

"Well, if we're lucky, this signal light is malfunctioning."

"And if we're unlucky?"

"We have a very serious problem."

*   *   *

Jerrold had always been the type of fellow who preferred to take his time in the washroom, but even so, he had been in there for an awfully long time. Carrie kept looking back at the lavatory door and saw that it was still shut. As the time passed, she started to worry that her husband had had an accident in there or worse—a heart attack.

She spoke to a passing stewardess when she could no longer stand waiting for him to return. "Excuse me, Miss, but my husband left to go to the washroom quite some time ago and he hasn't returned. I'm worried that something has happened to him."

At that moment, a man emerged from the cockpit. It was the copilot, Roy Bacus, sent to investigate the possibility that the plane's door had been opened sometime during the flight. He was moving purposefully while trying not to allow his swiftness to arouse suspicion, but before he could get to the back of the plane he was stopped by the stewardess who had just spoken to Carrie.

"What's wrong," she whispered to him, knowing something was up.

"A warning light is telling us that the door has somehow been opened."

The stewardess went white.

"What is it?" Roy asked when he noticed her reaction.

"A woman just told me that she's worried because her husband hasn't returned from the washroom. You don't think—"

"Oh God, I hope not," answered Roy. He moved as quickly as he could to the back of the plane. Near the lavatory he saw that the door was open, but only just enough

Mysterious things can sometimes happen on airplanes.

so that it would set off the warning signal. DC-3s don't require that their cabins be pressurized, so no one had noticed the small amount of air that was passing through the opening.

The stewardess walked over to him as he picked up a piece of chain from the cabin's floor.

"I've talked to everyone," she said. "No one has seen Mr. Potter since he left to go to the washroom and he's not there now," she confirmed by opening the vacant lavatory's door.

Roy returned to the cockpit to tell Miguel what was going on.

"You look like you've seen a ghost," said the head pilot when he saw him come back in. "Was the door open?"

"Yes, but that's nothing. We're missing a passenger," Roy told him.

"What?" Miguel turned from his controls, shocked by the news. "What happened?"

"I don't know," Roy said.

"What's that in your hand?"

Roy looked down at the piece of chain in his right hand. "I found this on the floor," he said. "It must have broken off the door when it was opened."

"Broken off? Do you think this guy tripped and slammed against the door and fell out?"

Roy shook his head. "No, the door was barely open— just enough to trigger the sensor."

"Maybe the air pressure caused it to close when he fell out?"

Roy reasoned with him. "But Miguel, this is a small plane. If something like that really happened, everyone in the cabin would have heard it and at least some of them would have seen it. No one heard or saw *anything*."

"No one?"

"No one."

From behind the cockpit door the two men could hear the sound of a woman screaming.

"Where's Jerrold?" she shouted. "Where is my husband? Somebody tell me what is going on! Where is he?"

Miguel landed the plane as soon as he could.

*   *   *

This is the bizarre story of a businessman named Jerrold Potter. Last seen on an airplane flying over the Ozarks, he vanished before the flight touched down in Springfield, Missouri. No one, including his wife, the plane's crew or the rest of its 21 passengers, had any explanation for what happened to him during that flight. One moment he was there, and then he was not.

An investigation began immediately. The investigators came up with a list of possible scenarios that could explain what happened during the flight and began going through them one by one to see if they fit the evidence.

The first possibility they studied was the one Miguel suggested to Roy while they were still in the air. Was it possible that Jerrold had tripped on the way to the washroom and hit the door hard enough for it to burst open and send him flying out into the air outside? The answer was no, it wasn't. Though the broken chain on the cabin floor indicated that such an impact occurred, it alone wouldn't have been sufficient to open the door, as the

How did Jerrold leave the plane?

mechanism required that the door's handle be turned 180 degrees before it became unlocked. This was not an easy thing to do. Often the process required the effort of two stewardesses to complete. There was simply no way a man of Jerrold's size could accidentally force the door open by slamming against it.

But what if it wasn't an accident? Could Jerrold have deliberately opened the door? This explanation was much more logical, but there was no evidence at all to support the idea that he was in any way suicidal. If anything, he was the happiest he had ever been in his life. But if he hadn't opened the door deliberately, did he become confused and think that it was the door to the washroom? That option seemed equally unlikely since he wasn't blind and was completely literate; there was no way he could have missed the large sign on the door warning passengers not to open it while the plane was in flight.

More and more suggestions were made, but each of them was shot down by one fact that could not be refuted.

Not one person on the plane had seen Jerrold go out the door. Not one. Considering the size of the plane and the noise that would have resulted if the door had opened wide enough for him to go through it, this was virtually impossible.

There were other explanations, but none of them were officially suggested, since they were the type of ideas that could get a person locked up if spoken aloud. One was that he was abducted by aliens. Another was that he had spontaneously combusted while he was in the bathroom and his ashes had disappeared into the toilet bowl. Then came the rumors that he had been the victim of the kind of vicious gremlins who had been said to cause all kinds of aircraft accidents. What if he was cursed? Or what if he really did die of a heart attack in the bathroom, just like Carrie had feared, and the crew and the company they worked for came up with the story that he disappeared to cover it up?

Carrie and her daughters sued Purdue Aviation, the company that owned the plane, but the case went nowhere. Unable to determine how or why he disappeared, her lawyers had no way to prove that the company was responsible. She held out hope that someday his body would be discovered somewhere in Missouri, but it never has.

To this day no ones knows what happened to Jerrold Potter on that flight in 1968. The mystery has never been solved and likely never will be, which is something for you to keep in mind the next time you travel by air—if you really have to go to the bathroom, make sure you take someone along to watch your back.

Patience's Pearl

It didn't take a psychic to know who was standing in the Curren's doorway, clacking the knocker with the kind of dedicated intensity usually only associated with humming-birds.

"Hello, Emily," Pearl mumbled as she opened the door and revealed her inexhaustible next-door neighbor.

Emily beamed at her happily. "Hi, Pearl. What are you doing?"

Pearl tried to think of something that she could say to indicate that she was incredibly busy and couldn't spare a second to entertain a guest. Unfortunately, Pearl had never been a quick thinker and Emily was fully aware that she had nothing but free time on her hands.

"I brought my Ouija board!" she exclaimed, while holding it out in front of her to prove the veracity of her statement.

Pearl rolled her eyes. The whole spirit world game had been exciting the first half-dozen times they played, but it became a lot less fun when she realized that the marker was being pushed by Emily wherever she wanted, instead of being guided by forces from the great beyond. She figured it out when it became clear that every single spirit somehow managed to misspell the same words over and over again. But John wasn't going to be home for another three hours and, with their maid taking care of all of the housework, she had nothing to do until then.

"Come on in," she said as Emily rushed into the house, giggling like a schoolgirl. "But this time, I'm doing the communing," she insisted.

Emily screeched to a halt. "But I always commune with the dead."

Pearl shrugged. "Not this time. I'm tired of being the secretary. You can take the dictation for a change."

Emily was not someone who could easily disguise her emotions. Her facial expressions shifted to and fro while she wrestled with this strange new development. Though disappointed, she finally agreed to Pearl's request. "Okay," she said while pouting, "but it's going to be a lot less fun if you do it. You don't have the same connection to the spiritual realm that I do."

"I don't doubt that," Pearl mumbled under her breath.

"What was that?" asked Emily.

"I don't know." Pearl turned and looked behind her. "Did you hear something I didn't? Maybe it was a trick of the wind?"

Emily shook her head. "No, it sounded like you mumbling something."

"Are you having one of your spells again, Emily? Should we skip the séance and get you to bed?"

"No," said Emily. "You're right. It was probably just the wind."

Pearl went to fetch some lemonade from the kitchen while Emily set up the board in the drawing room. She looked visibly uncomfortable when Pearl came in with their refreshments and took her seat in front of the board.

"Are you sure you know how to do it right?" Emily asked anxiously.

"Yes," Pearl answered and sighed. "I call out to the spirit world and ask them to guide the marker and answer all of our questions."

Emily frowned. "It's harder than it sounds," she insisted.

Pearl ignored her comment and decided to have some fun with her annoying acquaintance.

"Ohhhhhhh, spirits of the netherworld," she said, hamming it up. "Come to us, I beg of thee! I am your humble vessel, use me and my board to journey back from the darkest reaches of death and answer our vital questions!"

Emily shook her head. "You're not doing it right."

Pearl pretended she didn't hear her and started moving the peg across the board. She closed her eyes and moved it randomly. "It's coming already!" she shouted. "Quick! Write down what the spirit is telling us!"

Emily grabbed the nearby pad and pencil and started writing down the letters Pearl blindly pointed to. Pearl kept at it until she felt she had teased Emily enough.

"How's that gibberish for you?" she asked with a laugh when she stopped.

Emily didn't answer her. Instead she just stared mutely at the piece of paper in front of her.

"What?" asked Pearl. "It's just nonsense. I didn't try to spell anything."

"Many moons ago, I lived," Emily read aloud from the piece of paper. "Again I come. My name is Patience Worth. If thou shalt live, so shall I."

"What are you doing?" asked Pearl. "Are you making that up?"

She could tell by the look on Emily's face that she wasn't.

"Ohhhhhh, spirits of the netherworld, come to us, I beg of thee!"

*   *   *

If it had been up to her mother, Patience would not have been taught to read or write. She considered all books—save one—to be frivolous and could think of no reason any woman would ever need to read one. To her, a young girl's time would be much better spent learning how to cook, bake, sew, clean and, time willing, play a musical instrument. But, thankfully for Patience, her father took a different view. As far as he was concerned, poetry was a gift from God, and it horrified him to think that his daughter might be denied its glory, so he would sit down with Patience after she finished her chores and tutor her in the wonderful complexities of verse.

As she grew into womanhood, Patience succeeded in pleasing both of her parents. She inherited her mother's devotion to hard work and practicality and her father's love for literature. And, when she turned 16, both gifts proved invaluable when her parents took ill with scarlet fever. For a full year she alone took care of them. She comforted her mother by keeping their home as perfect and tidy as it always had been, and she soothed her father by reading to him his favorite poems—some of which she had composed herself.

They died within days of each other, leaving Patience alone in the world. Everything they had was sold to pay off the debts they had incurred during their convalescence. Patience was left with only £3 to her name and a suitcase full of old clothes. With the help of a family friend she got a job as a nanny for a businessman named Krelby who lived in the nearby town of Dorsetshire.

Krelby had five children, all of whom were pleasant, and the job would have been a fine one were it not for his wife, Vera. Patience had inherited her job from Vera, who had married her employer six months after his first wife's accidental death. They were both the same age and Vera viewed Patience as unwanted competition inside her home. Her insecurity was not unwarranted; Vera herself had been having an affair with Krelby long before his first wife had been so fortuitously (for Vera) thrown from her horse. It didn't help Patience that she was much more attractive than Vera was or that the children seemed to like her more than they did their stepmother. She was forced to swallow her pride as her jealous predecessor went out of her way to belittle her.

It was 1682, and Patience did not have the luxury of defending herself against Vera's acts of petty cruelty. She had no money, no family, no prospects for another job, and the thought of marrying one of the few eligible bachelors she knew at that time caused her to imagine inescapable futures even more dire than her present circumstances. So she devoted herself to the virtue for which she was named, accepted her plight and did her best to pretend that Vera did not exist.

But there was one place where she allowed herself the luxury of unrestrained expression. Every night, just before she went to bed, she would open up her journal and write until she could no longer remain awake. She wrote a lot about Vera, but she also filled the journal's pages with poetry and fiction that inspired her to continue even on the darkest of days. In fact, she entitled one of these poems "Is Thy Day Dark" and dedicated it to all those who labored under harsh conditions like herself. It read:

O my love, is thy day dark? Behold then, He is the sun.
Is thy day over bright? Then behold, He is the shadow.
Look unto the sky, the face of God,
The secret of the universe is there writ. Read!
Remember thee, remember, the folly of over much wisdom;
Remember, even wisdom is outdone by love.

She told no one of this journal's existence, and she kept it close to her at all times. The fear that she would someday lose it plagued her dreams. She knew that if her employers knew of some of the things she had written about them, they would throw her out onto the street without a second's hesitation. At times she grew so anxious that she considered throwing the journal away, but if she did that, she knew it would only be a matter of time before her patience gave out and she would do something to Vera that they both would regret.

Eleven years passed. At the beginning of each new year she would destroy the previous year's journal—saving only the most innocent of the poems it had contained—and start another. Time had been hard on her, and her beauty had been toughened by the hardships she withstood, but unfortunately the worst was yet to come.

On the eve of her 28th birthday, Mr. Krelby collapsed in his bedroom and died instantly of a sudden heart attack. His estate was passed down to his eldest son, Michael, who was not yet six, which meant it was in his mother's control. At first Patience thought her ex-employer's passing might make her life easier. With him gone, Vera had no reason to torment her, but this was not the case. Vera had grown so used to demeaning her nanny that it had become a habit she could not break. If anything, Mr. Krelby's absence gave her the chance to take her abuse to new extremes. Patience did her best to forge on, but then one day she walked into her tiny room and found Vera sitting on her bed with a book in her hands.

Horrified, she reached for the pocket in which she always kept her journal and discovered that it was empty.

"I found this in the hallway," Vera said with the journal in her hands. She sneered as she leafed through its pages. "I assumed it was yours."

For a moment Patience thought she was safe. Vera could not read, which meant that if she had found it and showed it to no one else, then she would have no idea about all of the horrible things its contents slandered her with.

"I do not pay you to waste your time with nonsense like this," Vera continued.

"I only write in it during my free time," Patience explained.

"Not anymore you don't!" Vera ordered. "If you have enough time to waste with something like this, I shall have to find more work for you to do."

"But I have to write."

"You have to do what I tell you to do if you want to stay in this house! It's up to you. Keep up writing whatever this nonsense is or find another job."

For Patience, the choice was simple.

*   *   *

Until that fateful afternoon at the Ouija board, Pearl's life had been one seemingly destined for mediocrity. She had been born Pearl Pollard in a nondescript Texas town in 1883, the daughter of simple folks whose lives were as average and boring as lives could be. She was neither homely nor pretty; people just considered her plain. She had not been raised to be intellectually curious, and she seldom read anything after she left school following the eighth grade. Her parents had never been very religious, so neither was she. She had never read the Bible and she knew virtually nothing about any matters spiritual.

For a time she thought about becoming a musician, but she was never serious about it. Instead, at the age of 24, she married an immigration official named John Curren and together they moved to St. Louis. There she lived a life of quiet boredom. While they were far from rich, John earned enough that they could afford to hire a maid to take care of all of their household needs, which left Pearl free to spend her time anyway she pleased. For many people this would seem a great blessing, but for someone like Pearl, who had no serious interests or hobbies, it meant that she spent most of her days taking naps and reluctantly playing card games with her neighbor Emily.

At first the Ouija board had been a nice change of pace, but it too became as boring as everything else for Pearl until that one afternoon. It was July 8, 1913. Pearl was 30 years old and finally her life was about to get interesting.

*   *   *

Left with nothing but her suitcase full of old clothes and her meager savings, Patience had spent a long night out walking the streets without a single idea about what she would do next. Her thoughts were so consumed with despair that she did not notice that the carriage that had been traveling down the street behind her came to a stop when it arrived right beside her.

"Ho there!" shouted a voice from the carriage.

Patience stopped and turned to see if these words had been meant for her.

From out of the carriage's side window she saw the face of Reginald Moulton, a wealthy gentleman who had been a regular guest in the Krelbys' home. She had always liked him. Despite his many riches he was that rare person who treated everyone equally regardless of their rank in life. Most of the people who visited the Krelbys had pretended as though she, or any of the other servants, did not exist, but Mr. Moulton actually knew them all by name.

"Aren't you a bit far from home, Patience?" he asked kindly.

"Not anymore, I'm afraid, Mr. Moulton, sir," she answered.

"How's that?"

"Mrs. Krelby left me with an ultimatum I could not accept, and so I was forced to leave her employ."

"And where was it she expected you to go?"

"I don't think she gave it much thought, sir."

"She's a horrid woman. I always thought so. I tried to convince Walter never to marry her, but he did not take my advice." He pondered this for a moment before he stood up and opened his carriage door. "Get in here, my dear, you look absolutely exhausted. Let's get you someplace warm."

Patience hesitated. "I wouldn't want to inconvenience you, sir."

"Nonsense! It is never an inconvenience for a man to do his Christian duty. Come, get in and we'll see if we can make your future a touch rosier than it is at present."

Unused to such generosity, Patience burst into tears.

"And we'll have none of that," Mr. Moulton chided her. "There is nothing so unsightly as a woman's tears."

"I'm sorry, sir." Patience wiped her tears away and stepped inside the carriage.

Once they reached Mr. Moulton's mansion, Patience was given some dinner and a place to sleep. Exhausted and relieved, she slept longer and deeper than she ever had before in her life. By the time she woke up, her life's course had already been profoundly changed. It was later, during afternoon tea (she had slept through breakfast), that her new benefactor told her about the great opportunity he had secured for her.

"I have a business acquaintance by the name of Dosh," he explained, "who has large holdings in the American colonies. For a time it was possible for him to oversee his interests from here in England, but last year it became evident that he would have to move to the new continent on a permanent basis. He left his wife and children behind, preferring to wait until he was properly settled before he sent word for them to join him. Well, that word has come, but Mrs. Dosh is too ill to make the journey. Still, she knows how much her husband loves his children and how much they miss him as well, so she is willing to pay quite generously for a woman with your experience to travel with her children to the colonies and serve as their nanny until she is well enough to make the journey on her own."

Patience couldn't believe her ears. She wasn't sure if the idea of traveling all the way to the New World was the most exciting or most frightening choice she had ever faced.

"Where is Mr. Dosh located?"

"One of the French territories. I can't recall its name. He trades goods with the local tribesmen who inhabit the area."

"Tribesmen? Do you mean Indians?"

"Yes, that's right."

This news tipped Patience slightly closer to the frightened side.

"But I've heard such horrible stories about them. I've heard that they are savages who know nothing of the ways of the Lord."

"Still," Mr. Moulton said, "that would make them a touch more hospitable than Mrs. Krelby."

Patience pretended to smile at this, but her fears had not been dissuaded.

"I would not worry about such things. These new colonies can be dangerous, I won't lie to you, but I suspect that they're a damn sight safer than being out alone on the street in Dorsetshire after nightfall."

"When would I have to leave?" she asked, still unsure if she would accept the offer or not.

"A month from today," he told her.

"A whole month? What shall I do until then?"

"Stay here as my guest, of course."

"But Mr. Moulton," she said, "I don't know what I have done to earn such kindness."

Mr. Moulton smiled. "That is not the issue," he told her. "A wiser person might wonder why I would feel the need to show such kindness. It is not a question I feel compelled to answer, but I will admit that my past has known enough shade that I believe it is in my best interest to do everything I can to enlighten it a touch."

Mr. Moulton did not force Patience to make her decision at that very moment, but by the end of the next day she had decided that—as frightening as it seemed to her—she was going to accept the offer and travel to a land she had never even dreamt about before. He was delighted to hear her acceptance and took it upon himself to secure all of the necessary arrangements. She met with Mrs. Dosh, who could not yet leave her bed, and with the three children she would accompany on the journey. The rest of her time was spent in Mr. Moulton's enormous library, where she wiled away the hours reading every book that caught her eye. In the next 30 days she read more than most people could expect to read in an entire lifetime, and with this new knowledge she started writing new poetry and began working on what she hoped would be an epic novel set in the biblical age. As she was set to leave on her incredible journey, she realized that refusing to accept Vera's ultimatum was the best decision she had ever made.

The constant seasickness that soon followed was enough to almost make her change her mind, but at least she knew her nausea would end once they reached land. Then, she hoped, her troubles would cease and her life would start feeling just a little normal again.

*   *   *

John had not been too impressed by Pearl's account of her strange message from the spiritual realm.

"What have I told you about wasting your time with such nonsense?" he said after she had finished excitedly telling him the story over dinner.

"It's not nonsense," she insisted. "It was very real. You should have seen the look on Emily's face. I swear I thought she was going to faint dead away."

John laughed. "I can't think of too many things that wouldn't astonish a mind as simply put together as Emily Hutching's," he said with a snort.

"Why do you make fun of everything I do?"

"Because you make it so easy for me," he answered. "Especially when you expect me to believe that you have actually spent the afternoon possessed by some spook from the great beyond."

"I expect you to believe me," she said angrily, "because that is what a good husband does."

"Wrong. A good husband has the sense to tell his wife when she is flirting with something that bears the scent of madness. It wouldn't do me any good to have you go crazy and end up in a straightjacket in the local looney bin."

"That's it." She pounded the table as she rose out of her chair. "I'm not talking to you anymore." Pearl left the dining room in a huff.

"Aw, Pearl…" he said wearily.

John had experienced enough of her passionate outbursts to know that her anger would fade quickly, but she still managed to make his life miserable for the short periods in which their fallout could be felt. He started to get up out his chair but stopped when she rushed back in holding Emily's Ouija board with a pad and pencil, which she forcefully placed on the table in front of him.

"What are you doing?" he asked.

Still not talking to him, she slid the pad and pencil in front of him and then sat down in front of the board.

"If you expect—" John started to say, but Pearl's angry glare suggested that he humor her for just this one moment.

She closed her eyes and placed her hands on the marker. For a full minute her hands did not move, but then the marker sprang to life, pointing out letters at such a rapid pace that John had difficulty recording them. The marker went on for 10 minutes before Pearl finally stopped.

"Well, what does it say?" she said, exhausted from what she had just received.

John had been so busy trying to keep up with her that he had not been able to decipher any meaning from what he had been writing. He looked down, expecting to find a mess of indecipherable rubbish, but as he scanned through the lines he had written on the pad he discovered not only that were there words in the passage, but also that several were words he knew were beyond the reaches of his wife's vocabulary. He never would have thought Pearl was capable of creating something like this.

"It's a poem," he told her.

"Really? Read it to me."

"What do you mean? You're the one who wrote it, you should know what it says."

"Patience wrote it," Pearl sighed wearily. "I just moved the marker."

John couldn't tell if she was having some fun at his expense or not, but he decided to read the poem anyway.

"A Message," he read aloud. "I guess that's the title," he added before clearing his throat and continuing. "Be there aught sae wondrous as a cup of communion? As a cup of fellowship? Be there aught sae wondrous to a wench as a right to wield her tongue, and good listeners? Be there aught sae wondrous as the fact that we may never, never, in the days to come, be separate? For I have become a part of thee, and thou hast become a part of me! This is an holy sacrament!"

"Is that what it really says?" asked Pearl when it was clear that he had finished.

"Yes," he answered, amazed by how genuine her surprise seemed to be.

"What do you think it means?"

"I think," he said, "it means that this Patience woman plans to stay here for a while."

*   *   *

If Patience had known that the journey to this place called Missouri would be this treacherous, she never would have agreed to it. It would have been a difficult task all by herself, but to do it while caring for three children made it almost impossible. She wondered what kind of man this Mr. Dosh could be that he would willingly allow his children to be subjected to the harsh miseries that came hand in hand with traveling across this long continent. Either he was a very cruel man, or his separation from them had driven him mad and desperate for their company, no matter what the cost.

Her only solace came from the time the long trip allowed her to write in her journal. While she suffered the many indignities of travel, she thought back to the turns her life had taken to get her into this situation and was inspired to write a poem called "The Little Grey Road." It went like this:

A little grey road that lies mid the shadows,
And trails from the Then to Now;
Where the briar-rose swings and the eve-lark sings,
And the dew clings 'bout the meadow way;
Where the sun lingers lothful, and the moon
Tarries too, so late to leave and soon to come.

Ah, the little grey roadway so far, far away,
Where I left my youth, treading with gladness,
And smiling, with bright hours to follow;
With no remembrance packed, like the scent
Of pale leaf that dropped at the withering touch
Of tears and sobs and sorrows.
All carefree I went, all happy a treading
On the little grey roadway so far.

Oh, that my feet might stray back
Through the fields and vales, and find
The same roadway a-roaming the shadows,
With memory's ghosts haunting the turns.
When the New Day doth come, and I leave
Thee and thee—shall I find it still waiting—
The little grey roadway wrapped in its shadows,
And my youth a-laughing me there?

She had written it while traveling in the back of a covered wagon, just 100 miles away from their final destination. It was the last poem she wrote while she was still alive.

*   *   *

Two weeks after the first breakthrough, the connection between Pearl and her Ouija board spirit was so strong that they no longer needed the board to communicate. Patience was now able to speak through Pearl, who often had to have someone else explain to her what the spirit had said. This wasn't because the spirit completely took over her body—she was always fully aware of everything Patience said—but was instead the result of the fact that Patience had a tendency to say things that completely went over Pearl's head.

"She insists on always using these big words," she said to visitors. "I don't know who she is trying to impress."

Patience, in turn, took occasional sport in mocking her medium's educational deficits. Sometimes she would stop in mid-sentence and explain to Pearl what one of these "big words" meant, or she would tease her host by deliberately making references she knew the simple woman had no hope of ever understanding.

Those who knew Pearl before she made this strange otherworldly connection were astounded by the phrases they heard coming out of her mouth. Even those who had been extremely skeptical of the news were unable to think of any other explanation for it when they met Patience.

"Either it's the real deal," said one acquaintance of hers, "or she has spent years pretending to be a nitwit just so she could pull this con off, and I honestly don't think she's smart enough to have been able to pretend to be stupid for that long."

Patience, at first, was too excited to have a voice to waste time telling anyone her life story, choosing instead to compose new poems and other literary works. She did, however, tell a gathering of Pearl's peers about the day that she died.

"It was a horrible day," she told everyone. "As hot as any I have ever encountered. I was sitting in the back of a covered wagon when I heard the sound of galloping hooves and loud cries. 'Indians!' cried out the wagon master. We were under attack! Arrows pierced through the canvas around me and one pierced the heart of the master, who dropped his reigns. The horses panicked and caused the wagon to flip over. I was thrown to the ground and saw a savage man gallop on a monstrous steed toward me. He held up a fearsome looking weapon and brought it down to my head and struck the life out of me. It was as frightening an encounter as any child of God could ever dare face."

What Patience did not know was that the men who had attacked her wagon were not Indians but French thieves disguised as such to shift blame away from them. Beyond that, it happened pretty much the way that she described it.

*   *   *

When it was suggested to Pearl that she try to get some of Patience's poems published, she seemed a bit surprised by the idea.

"Are they really good enough for that sort of thing?" she wondered aloud.

It turned out that they were.

Within a month the first of Patience's poems were printed, and their publisher eagerly asked for more.

Though they were all published under Patience's name, no one yet knew that the credited authoress had been deceased since the 17th century. It wasn't until the news of this bizarre story reached a journalist named Casper Yost, who wrote a book about Pearl and Patience entitled *Patience Worth: A Psychic Mystery*, that the writing duo became more popular.

This newfound acceptance for her work only made Patience more ambitious. She put aside her poetry for a time and set to work, dictating through Pearl the biblical epic she had always dreamed of writing. She called it *The Sorry Tale*, and the book was published to rave reviews. One critic went so far as to suggest that it was the best work written about the period since the gospels.

Having written an epic smash with *The Sorry Tale*, Patience decided to try something even more ambitious and wrote the shorter, but much more complex, novel, *Telka: A Medievel Idyll*. She wrote it in less than two days and composed much of it in iambic pentameter. Even those who were still skeptical over Patience's existence had to admit that if it were a hoax, it was an elaborately well-researched one. Not once in the course of the book's 70,000 words did Patience use a word that did not exist before her death.

The depth and complexity of these books went a long way to dispel the notion that Pearl was a fraud. And many believed, even if she was, the popular and critical acceptance of the work she published served to mitigate any speculation that she had created Patience as a way of selling her own writing. Even if Patience didn't really exist, the work was still good enough to merit the attention it was receiving.

Still, some in the Curren household didn't take kindly to the idea that Patience was a figment of Pearl's imagination, namely Patience herself, who was deeply insulted that anyone would think that a common housewife with a barely acceptable vocabulary could have ever created the work in question. As a way for Patience to combat this perception, skeptics were allowed to visit the Currens and asked to suggest a topic of their choice for a poem. Within seconds Patience would begin to dictate a new poem on that very subject, and an hour or so after its creation— to prove that Pearl hadn't simply created gibberish on the spot—she would give a word for word recitation of the poem.

Sometimes lost among all the creative hubbub was Pearl, who often played second to her talented other half. Wanting a little attention for herself, she decided to try her own hand at writing and eventually managed to publish several short stories for children in the *Saturday Evening Post*. Patience took a very patronizing attitude toward Pearl's solo literary efforts, but Pearl remained extremely proud of them; it proved that she was more than just a famous ghost's connection to the real world.

Their relationship was already at odds due to Patience's increasing disdain toward her host, but it really took a turn for the worse in 1922, nine years after they had first come together, when Pearl became pregnant. Upon the birth of her baby, she had little time to deal with Patience's needs and the two of them connected less and less frequently.

As they grew apart, the literary world was changing. The style of Patience's writing was now out of fashion; her work ceased to be published, and her books went out of print.

Despite her waning popularity, Patience remained with Pearl and composed several more poems before Pearl's death in 1937.

The Curse

Hadley Reed was a man without a home. The war was over and his side had won, but the Union's victory did little to salve the wounds he had suffered in Lincoln's war. His wife and children were killed in a Rebel attack where no one was spared. His ranch was burned to the ground, his livestock was stolen and killed and his crops were destroyed, leaving him with nothing but a few dollars to his name and his horse. Wearing an old suit (he could no longer bear to wear his uniform) Hadley rode along the Missouri River, hoping to find somewhere to begin a new life.

It was not a time when strangers were welcomed into people's lives; Hadley wasn't the only person whose soul had been wounded in the great conflict, and most of these injured spirits were no longer capable of acts of charity or kindness. The people he met were not happy to see him. No one offered him a roof for the night or a meal to eat.

He spent his days sleeping on the ground and eating only what nature would provide. His hair grew long and his beard became matted. He stopped looking like the gentleman farmer he once was and started looking like the kind of mountain man or hermit that people warned others to avoid. A part of him feared he would no longer be a member of proper society ever again, while another part of him didn't really care if he ever spoke to another person for as long as he lived.

As he rode into a town, he no longer made any attempt to talk to anyone, choosing instead to simply keep riding.

He knew that at some point he would have to stop and settle in one of these towns, but he had no idea where or when.

He had never heard of Booneville, and he had intended to ride through it the same way he had the past dozen other towns he had encountered along his journey, but something made him stop and he ended up living there for the rest of his life.

The whole 13 days.

*　　　*　　　*

It was, by far, the worst night he had spent outside since before the war. The rain was coming down so hard that it felt as though God had taken an ocean and was deliberately spilling it onto the land. He was so wet that he could no longer comprehend what it felt like to be dry. There was no hiding from it—unless you were in a fortress or a castle, there was simply no way to avoid getting wet.

This was easily the most uncomfortable and miserable that Hadley had ever been in his life. Had a madman kidnapped him and spent hours subjecting him to the worst kind of tortures the human mind could ever conceive of, it is highly unlikely he would have felt the slightest bit worse.

For the first time in his life, his thoughts drifted toward suicide.

But before these dark thoughts could fester inside his mind, he saw a light in the distance. Even through the rain he could see that it came from a lantern in a far-off window. He figured that the owner of the home might be dubious

It felt as though God had taken an ocean and was deliberately spilling it onto the land.

about letting him inside, but he decided to try anyway—
a chance was better than not trying at all.

It took him an hour to reach the light, and when he
did he could not believe what he had found.

It was a castle.

*   *   *

Hadley's eyes were deceiving him; the building wasn't
actually a castle, but a mansion, long-deserted and left
to rot. It was an honest mistake because it was as close to
a castle a person could expect to find in the state of
Missouri. It looked as though it had been years since anyone had cared for it, but the light shining in the second-
floor corner window strongly suggested that the mansion
was occupied.

Barely able to move, thanks to the weight of his rain-
soaked clothes, he jumped off his horse with a tremendous splash, tied the waterlogged creature to a post and
slogged his way to the building's front door. He tried to
open the heavy oak door but it was locked. Desperate
to get inside, he started banging on the door as hard as he
could. Out of the corner of his eye he saw the light in the
window flicker and fade. He moved away from the door
and saw that the light was now gone. He waited.

"Who is it?" he heard a voice, barely audible, from
behind the door.

"My name is Hadley Reed," he answered. "I've been in
this rain for a very long time and I need some shelter."

There was a pause as the person behind the door considered what to do next.

The door opened and Hadley almost fell over when he saw who had been behind it.

The woman held a lamp in her right hand and its flame caused light to flicker across her face. She was around his age—maybe slightly younger. Her hair was long and dark and her eyes were green. She wore a thin white nightdress, and she shivered as the cold air from outside touched her lightly freckled skin. She was as beautiful a woman as he had ever seen.

"You better come in," she said, her voice barely rising above a soft whisper. She turned around and disappeared in the house's darkness. Hadley followed her inside and closed the door behind him. It was so dark inside that he could barely see her walking in front of him. She had a slightly eerie aura as she started walking up the stairs in the dim light. Hadley wondered how he could have seen such a light from so far away in the rain when he could barely see it when it was just a few steps ahead of him.

"You must be very uncomfortable," she said as she continued up the stairs.

"Yes, ma'am," he answered. "I can't recall the last time I've been *this* wet."

"I have some of my father's old clothes hanging in a closet. They should fit you, I think."

"That would be ideal, ma'am. My clothes have gotten so heavy I can barely make my way up these steps."

The two of them reached the top of the stairs and the woman turned and entered the first room they came across. Even in the dark, he could see that everything in the room was covered in a thick layer of dust and spiderwebs.

"I take it you don't visit this room too often," he said jokingly to the kind woman.

"No," the woman admitted. "I haven't been in this room for 20 years. Not since my father died." She opened up the room's closet and held up the lamp to illuminate a row of fine suits. "I suppose the moths have eaten their fill of these by now, but I suspect we can find a wearable combination if we look for it."

She started looking through the closet while Hadley stood and dripped behind her. She stopped and looked at him. "Now isn't the time for modesty," she told him. "I suggest you get out of those clothes before you catch a fever."

Hadley didn't need to be told twice. He started stripping out of his wet clothes as quickly as he could, while the woman continued to look for something he could wear. Each piece of clothing he removed hit the ground with heavy splat. By the time the last of them hit the floor, the woman had an outfit ready for him.

"There are a few holes here and there in these, but they should keep you warm for the rest of the night."

"Thank you, ma'am," he said gratefully.

"You're welcome," she answered back.

"Considering the depth of your generosity," he said to her as he started putting on the old clothes, "I hate to admit that I have one more thing to ask of you."

"What's that?" she asked.

"Your name."

She looked at him directly and revealed a small smile before turning away. "It's Nancy," she told him. "Nancy Muir."

*   *   *

Nancy lit another lamp and gave it to Hadley. She then showed him to a room that was much less dusty than her father's and left him to rest for the night. It was the first time he had slept in a bed in over a year. He fell asleep in an instant and was awakened only when the sun started shining through the windows into his eyes. He felt like he wanted to stay in bed for the rest of his life, but he decided to get up and thank his hostess for her wonderful hospitality.

In the light of day the mansion proved to be even more impressive and frightening than it looked during the night. The work throughout the mansion was extremely ornate and must have cost a fortune when it was built, but it now looked outdated and damaged from years of neglect. It was obvious that Nancy thought little about homemaking and had neither the will nor ability to keep the mansion from falling apart.

He ended up seeing most of the mansion before he found her in the kitchen, preparing a simple breakfast for the two of them. She gave him a cup of coffee and ladled some porridge for him into a bowl.

"I'm going to have to do something to pay you back for all of this," he told her as he accepted the food.

"That won't be necessary."

"I insist."

"That's very honorable of you," she said, "but it's not a good idea for you to stay around the mansion. It is not a safe place to live."

"You seem to have survived," he answered back.

"I am immune to its dangers," she said in her customary whisper.

"Perhaps I am too."

Once again, as it had the previous night, a smile came close to appearing on her lips before she forced it to go away. "I wish that were true," she told him, "but it is not that simple. Everything that lives here dies. Everything except me."

"I'm sure you're exaggerating."

"I wish I were."

*   *   *

Hadley did not heed his hostess' wishes. Instead he went outside and inspected the mansion's grounds. In the back was an abandoned stable where he found his horse. Nancy must have let the animal in sometime while he was sleeping. As he started walking back to the mansion he caught a glimpse of his reflection in a puddle on the ground, and he couldn't believe that she let him into her home looking the way he did.

"Did your father have a shaving kit?" he asked her when he returned.

"Of course," she answered him. She disappeared for a few minutes before returning with an expensive-looking leather bag, which she handed over to him.

The bag's contents were all fashioned out of ivory and silver. The razor was dull with age, but Hadley found a sharpening stone among the items in his pack.

"Your family must have been very wealthy," he said to Nancy as he worked on honing the razor's edge.

"We did all right," she admitted modestly.

"Was it the war?" he asked her.

"Pardon me?"

"Was it the war that split your family apart? Is that why you're alone in this gigantic house?"

"I don't know what you're talking about. There was a war?"

"You're joking, right?"

"About what?"

"The war. The war that took everything I had. The war that nearly swallowed this country whole."

"I don't get out much," she told him.

"Don't get out much?" He couldn't believe his ears. "You would have to be dead to not know about the war between the North and the South."

"I am many things," she insisted, "but I assure you that dead is not one of them."

*   *   *

After shaving his beard, Hadley almost didn't recognize the man behind it as he stared at his reflection in the mirror. "I look a lot younger," he told Nancy when he was done.

"You're very handsome."

"Thank you." He looked at her and smiled. "You're not too hard to look at yourself."

"Really? Am I pretty?"

Hadley thought she was teasing him. "Of course you are," he told her. "And don't try to pretend otherwise.

People must have complimented you for your beauty all your life."

"It's been a long time," she admitted. "I thought maybe something changed since then."

*   *   *

Though she was never rude or inhospitable, Hadley quickly got the sense that Nancy genuinely wanted him to leave, not because she didn't like having him around, but because she sincerely feared for his safety. Ironically this is what made it so hard for him to go. He could not bring himself to leave before he learned the truth about this beautiful recluse—a woman who was so cut off from the world outside the mansion that she hadn't even known that her country had been at war with itself for the last several years.

He had been there three days when his horse became ill. Though he was far from being a veterinarian, he had cared for enough horses on his ranch to know that the condition was serious and that the animal was unlikely to live until the end of the day. He was caring for the poor creature when he heard Nancy's voice behind him.

"Your horse is dying," she said in her trademark whisper. "I told you that this is a place of death. Nothing here lives for long."

"You've done all right."

"Have I?" she asked. "Is it all right to watch helplessly as everything you love withers and dies around you?"

Hadley thought of everything he had lost during the past year. "No, it isn't all right. It is wrong—as wrong as anything could ever hope to be. I'm sorry that I suggested otherwise."

"Don't apologize. You don't know what happened."

"You could tell me."

She bit her lip and thought for a moment. "No, I couldn't," she answered.

A few hours later, Hadley's horse died.

*   *   *

He didn't know what to do next. Without a horse, he was now going to have to travel by foot. The town of Booneville was only a few miles away but he had no money and it was unlikely he would find anyone there who would be willing to take him in. He could tell that Nancy enjoyed his company, but the longer he stayed the more anxious she became—as if she truly believed that he was going to die there if he didn't leave soon.

The thought of all of this kept him awake at night. Unable to sleep, he got up and lit his lamp and started wandering around the house, walking quietly so as not to disturb his hostess.

Barely able to see, with only the lamp's small flame flickering in front of him, he found himself in a room downstairs he had never been in before. It appeared to be a storage room filled with all kinds of different things. He was only five steps into the room before he stubbed his toe on one of these items. It was a small chest. He bent over and opened it. In it he found the kind of trinkets that would be important to a young girl—a small doll, some silver charms and a long silk scarf.

He could not bring himself to go before he learned the truth about this beautiful recluse.

"You shouldn't be in here," he heard Nancy whisper behind him.

"I'm sorry," he apologized, "I couldn't sleep. I didn't mean to intrude."

"It's no intrusion," she told him. "It's just that it can be dangerous in this room at night. I only come in during the day, when I can see everything in the sunlight."

"Is this yours?" he held up the scarf.

"It was," Nancy told him. "A long time ago. It's some-one else's now."

"Are they coming back for it?" he asked.

"Only if they're planning on returning from the grave," she answered. "They've been dead for 20 years now."

"Then I don't think they would mind if you took it back," he said.

"They can keep it," she insisted. "I have no use for silk scarves these days."

*   *   *

Hadley had been at the mansion for 10 days when Nancy finally became concerned enough about his continued safety to insist that he leave.

"But I don't understand," he said to her. "I know you like having me around. I can tell how lonely you were before I arrived. Why are you so adamant that I go?"

Nancy sighed, close to the edge of tears. "How many times must I tell you before you believe me? You think I am this crazy lonely woman, but I'm not. I know how happy it would make me if you could stay, but if you do not leave right now, you will die in this house."

"You keep saying that but you refuse to tell me why it's so."

"Because that is what happens here," she said through her tears. "Everything in or near this house dies. Everything except me."

"I'm sure something happened to you that makes it feel as though that were true, but that's all it is—a feeling.

This house is not cursed. You are not cursed. There is no such thing in this world as a curse."

"If I could believe that I would not be telling you to go."

"Then believe it."

Nancy wiped away her tears and looked at him with an expression of absolute determination. For the first time since he had arrived her voice was louder than just a whisper. "It's not that simple, Hadley," she said to him. "Get out of this house. Now! And never come back."

At that moment he could tell that nothing he could say or do would convince her to change her mind, so he just nodded and walked out the mansion's front door.

*   *   *

It took him four hours to walk to Booneville. During the walk he felt something in one of his pockets. He reached inside and found some old bills, which though old, were still legal tender as far as he could tell. Nancy must have slipped him the money sometime before she forced him to leave. There was enough to last him for a couple of weeks—which was hopefully enough time for him to find some work.

But first he needed a place to stay. Many of the houses he walked past had signs advertising for boarders. He chose one at random and knocked on the door. The old woman who answered it seemed eager to take him in. Times were tough and she could use all of the extra money she could get. She asked him if he was hungry and offered to cook him dinner. He agreed and as she prepared their meal, he sat at her kitchen table and took some time getting to know his new landlady.

Midway through their conversation, she asked him about the clothes he was wearing. "That was a fine suit in the day," she told him. "You hardly see its like anymore. Where did you find it?"

"It's a bit moth eaten," he admitted, "but it doesn't look half bad if I say so myself. A woman I met gave them to me. They once belonged to her father."

"He must have been a wealthy man to own a suit as fine as that."

"She lives in a mansion."

"We don't have many of those around here," the old woman said. "Just the old haunted Muir place down the river's path."

"Excuse me?" Hadley sat up in his chair, taken aback by the woman's choice of words. "What did you just say?"

"Just that the only mansion we have around Booneville is the old Muir place."

"Yes, I got that, but you also said it was—" the word wanted to stay in his mouth—"haunted?"

"That's because it is. Has been for 20 years. Ever since that slave cursed the whole family when she was caught stealing something from their youngest daughter."

"Nancy?"

"That's right," the old woman nodded. "So you know the story?"

Hadley shook his head. "No, I don't. Tell it to me, please."

*   *   *

Nancy kept all of her most prized possessions in the chest in her room. In it she kept her doll and her silver charms and, most importantly, the silk scarf her grandmother had given her during her last visit just before she died. Everyday she would open the chest and make sure that all of her treasures were safe and secure. She had no idea what she would do if she ever actually found something missing, and she dreaded the idea that that day would ever come.

And then it did.

It had been a warm day and she had spent it playing outside. Charity, one of the family's slaves, called out to tell her that dinner was almost ready, so she had to get inside and change clothes or risk the ire of her stern mother. Nancy heeded Charity's warning and came in and headed to her room. Across the hallway she saw the oldest of the slaves—a strong, intimidating woman named Aunt Eternity—leaving her bedroom. This was odd to Nancy because Aunt Eternity's duties usually kept her in the front parlor, so she had no cause to be in her room.

The first thing Nancy did when she got inside her room was open her chest, and—just as she feared—something was missing.

It was the silk scarf.

Nancy ran to tell her father what had happened. He confronted Aunt Eternity in the hut she called home behind the mansion and found the scarf, which he returned to his daughter. Aunt Eternity was demoted to scullery maid, where she could be watched much more closely.

A week later, Nancy became sick.

A doctor was sent for, but he did little to stop her fever.

Her father paid for a specialist to come all the way from St. Louis, but he too could do nothing to stop the fever.

Nancy was not long for this world.

Her father despaired that even with his great wealth he could do nothing to save the life of his little girl. Of all the things that could ever happen to him, losing Nancy would be—by far—the worst. It felt as though someone was trying to punish him, and his instincts led him to exactly who it was.

Working in the kitchen, Aunt Eternity was able to poison Nancy's food. It was her revenge for being exposed as a thief and for the demotion that followed.

Blind with rage, Nancy's father grabbed a bullwhip and ran to Aunt Eternity's hut. She was so terrified by the look on his face that she collapsed before he could land a single blow. Just before her heart stopped she gasped out a curse—she proclaimed that the future of the Muirs would know only misery and pain.

*   *   *

"What happened to the Muirs after that?" Hadley asked the old woman.

"They were all dead within a year. It was as if a plague had descended on the mansion. All of the animals died first and then the slaves. Then Nancy passed on, followed by her mother. Mr. Muir was the last one to survive. He shot himself when the despair became too powerful for him to take. After that people kept away from the mansion—it's a place where death is far too welcome to a visitor."

Hadley had heard enough. He reached into his pocket and pulled out some money and left it on the woman's table. He then got up and left the house and started running back to the mansion he had been forced to leave just that morning.

*   *   *

He found Nancy in the kitchen.

"Are you a ghost?" he asked.

"Do I look like one?"

"I don't know, you might."

"Then you talked to one of the locals," she guessed. "They told you about the curse."

"Yes."

"They told you that I died. And you believed them?"

"Yes."

"You shouldn't have. They don't know what they're talking about. Aunt Eternity didn't curse my father," she explained. "She cursed me. I lived. I lived to see everyone I loved die."

"It must have been horrible."

"More than you can ever know."

"But that was 20 years ago."

She shook her head. "No, the curse remains. I told you, this is a place of death and it always will be as long as I am alive."

"You can't believe that."

She turned away from him. "Yes, I can. You think you are the first stranger to walk through those doors? There have been others. Not many but enough for me to know for certain that anyone who gets to know me is doomed. That's why you have to leave and never come back. I can't be responsible for another person's death."

The silence that followed lasted a long time before Hadley knew what to say.

"It's not your responsibility," he told her. "It's mine."

"What are you saying?"

"I'm saying that I know the consequences of staying here. And I would rather spend my last days on earth with you than live another 30 years alone."

*   *   *

Hadley took ill on the 12th day.

Nancy knew he would not recover.

He didn't.

And she buried him along with the others.

2
Haunted Buildings

Sarah's Rebel

It was the middle of the morning, a few hours before lunch. Sarah had left her math homework inside the small dorm room she shared with her best—and only—friend Margaret. When she stepped into the room she felt a tingle up her spine, as if her body was preparing for a shock it sensed was on its way. Before she could give the sensation the benefit of a thought, she discovered that it was not simply a trick of her nervous system, but rather a very real warning—one that had come far too late.

She felt a hand grab her across her mouth. It was rough and bloody and strong, and it kept her from screaming. Another hand, attached to a long, sinewy arm wrapped around her chest and kept her from struggling. On her cheek she felt the warmth of another person's breath. The smell of it made her eyes water. It stank of rotten meat.

"Don't you scream, girl," said a man's voice, sounding much more frightened than threatening. "All you'll do is get a dying man killed before he's ready to go."

Sarah began to cry, but she did not make a sound.

When the man finally released her, Sarah turned and saw a handsome young soldier, not much older than she was, dressed in a torn and dirty Confederate uniform. He had not shaved in weeks and his face and arms were covered with mud and what appeared to be his own blood. He had tied a rag around his right leg as a makeshift tourniquet to staunch the flow from a wound that looked to be only a few hours old. At once all of Sarah's fear turned into empathy for the man.

"Lay down," she ordered him, pointing over to her bed.

He looked at her as if he was trying to determine the nature of her intentions.

"Just do it," she barked at him impatiently.

He snapped to attention, hobbled over to the bed and collapsed on top of it. Sarah bent over him and started stripping him out of his clothes.

"What are you doing?" he asked, shocked by her actions.

"I'm getting you out of these clothes so I can see how badly you're hurt," she told him impatiently.

He accepted her logic and allowed her to remove his uniform. She was working on his pants when the door to the room opened without any warning.

Sarah's roommate, Margaret, was a calm, quiet girl, the kind of person who was good in an emergency because of her ability to immediately accept strange situations and react to them without becoming hysterical. But even she was taken aback by the sight of her friend removing the pants of a handsome, well-built young man.

She paused in the middle of the doorway, her brain clearly unable to process the bizarre tableau unfolding in front of her. "Uh…"

"Close the door!" Sarah yelled at her. "Before someone sees anything!"

"Right," said Margaret as she did as she was told. With the door closed she just stood there and gaped openly as Sarah finished stripping the young soldier of the last of his clothes.

"Don't just stand there like a jackass," Sarah grumbled. "Come over here and help me."

This last request was just what it took to break Margaret out of her reverie.

"Sarah," she said, "there's a man in your bed."

"I know," Sarah answered her.

"A *naked* man."

"I know," she answered again.

"I'm going to need an explanation," Margaret insisted. The young man took the opportunity to explain. "Ma'am, my name is Corporal Isaac Johnson. I was injured while on a covert mission here in Columbia and I had to act quickly to escape detection from those that injured me. I climbed into that window there and your friend is being kind enough to help me."

"Is that true, Sarah?"

Sarah shrugged. "All I know is that he was in here when I came in to get my homework and he looked like he needed help. Now quit asking stupid questions and go fetch Ruby."

Margaret hesitated. "Sarah..."

"Do it now! He's bleeding bad and I don't want him dying on my bed!"

Margaret didn't question her again. Instead she turned and ran out the door, heading toward the school's kitchen.

"Ruby?" asked Isaac.

"She'll help us. She's a thousand times better than any doctor. You'll see," Sarah explained. "Are you thirsty?"

He nodded. She went over to a pitcher she and Margaret always kept full on their dresser and poured him a glass of water.

"Here," she said as she held the cup up to his mouth, "take small sips."

Isaac sipped carefully from the cup and looked at the young woman in front of him. If there was such a thing as the perfect person to find you when you were on the lam from the Union soldiers who shot you in the leg when they caught you attempting to steal one of their fallen compatriot's uniforms, then this girl was it. To his eyes she was the most beautiful woman in the world. This judgment, in truth, had more to do with the long months he had spent at war—absent from the blessing of female beauty—than it did Sarah's natural charisma. She was a pretty girl, but hardly beautiful in the traditional sense of the word. For the moment, however, Isaac was only too happy to take her in.

"Do I have something on my face?" she asked him when she caught him staring at her.

"No, sorry. It's just been a long time."

"Since what?"

"Since I saw such a pretty girl."

Sarah blushed, but before she could say anything back to him, Margaret ran into the room followed quickly by a small, middle-aged black woman.

"Ruby, it's his leg," Sarah explained to the older woman.

"I can see that, Miss Sarah," Ruby responded.

"Can you stop the bleeding?" asked Isaac.

"I don't see why not," Ruby said. She told the girls exactly what she would need to make that happen.

Sarah hadn't been exaggerating. Ruby really did know more about healing people than most doctors, and within half an hour Isaac's wounds had stopped bleeding and were properly bandaged. His ordeal had proven so exhausting that by the time she was finished he was already fast asleep.

"Now Ruby, you have to promise me that you won't tell anyone about our visitor," Margaret said.

"I won't, Miss Margaret," Ruby agreed. "This'll be between us and the Lord, that's all."

"That's right. Now you better get back to the kitchen. It's almost lunchtime."

Ruby nodded and disappeared out the door.

"I know we can trust her," Sarah said.

Margaret shrugged. "It doesn't really matter because it's only a matter of time before someone discovers him anyway. People are looking for him, Sarah. He must've done something serious to make that happen."

"We only need a couple of days," Sarah said reassuringly. "By then he'll be healthy enough to make his escape."

"Are you sure?"

"For his sake and ours, I hope so," Sarah answered her.

*   *   *

When the Columbia Female Academy was founded in 1833, it was the first school of its kind in the state of Missouri. The dream of Colonel Richard Gentry, it came to be because many of Columbia's most prominent men desired to see their daughters receive a proper education. Over the years the school grew from a 25-girl class taught in a local Presbyterian church into the much larger Stephens Female College, and during that time the school earned a reputation as a good place for parents to send their daughters to be educated without the distraction of young men.

Even before the war, men had been a rare sight at the college. Along with the school's president, Dr. Hubert Williams, there were only a handful of male faculty members, none of whom were likely to capture the interest of their young pupils. As a result, any young man who happened to have business at the school—be it to make a delivery or to perform some repairs—would find himself suddenly surrounded by attractive young women who were inexplicably fascinated with his every move.

And once the war started, the sight of a man, who was not part of the faculty, at Stephens College became as rare as a sugar, which was also in very short supply. For a romantically inclined young woman like Sarah June Wheeler, this was nothing short of the worst kind of torture. Her interest in boys had been a major reason why her parents sent her to the college in the first place, a fact made obvious by her total lack of interest in anything that resembled higher learning. Naturally distrustful of other girls, she made no attempts to make any friends among her peers, with the exception of her roommate, Margaret Baker.

Margaret was from Arkansas, and in terms of appearance, was very different from her roommate. She was short and squat, while Sarah was tall and willowy. Her hair was dark, while Sarah's was honey blond. Her eyes were brown, and Sarah's were a piercing blue. But despite their physical differences, they were very much the same person. Both were prone to flights of whimsical fancy and liked to imagine they were heroines in the kind of novels that their professors frowned upon.

They were, in short, the only two girls at the college who—upon finding a wounded Confederate soldier in their room—wouldn't immediately report his presence to Dr. Williams. Whether it was fate or luck, Isaac had chosen exactly the right window to climb into that morning.

The reason he was forced to make this fortuitous decision was because he had foolishly volunteered for a mission with which he believed he could earn a small sliver of revenge. It started when he had been captured at the Battle of Pea Ridge. From there he had been sent to a prison camp in Illinois. With a mixture of equal parts cunning and dumb luck, he managed to escape from the prison and make his way back to a Confederate outpost. It was there where he saw a list of casualties the Rebels had suffered in an attack on Nashville, and among those names was his father's. Torn apart with grief, he immediately agreed to accept what many believed to be a suicide assignment. He was to go to Columbia, Missouri, and assassinate General Henry Halleck, who had recently wrested control of the town away from the Confederate army.

Isaac had made it safely all the way to Columbia, but his plan was almost immediately foiled when he was caught trying to steal a uniform off a dead Union soldier. He was fired at and wounded, but he managed to avoid being captured and hobbled his way to a nearby building, which he entered through an open window.

Beyond finding the only two girls who would be sympathetic to his plight, there was another reason he had been incredibly fortunate to pick this particular window

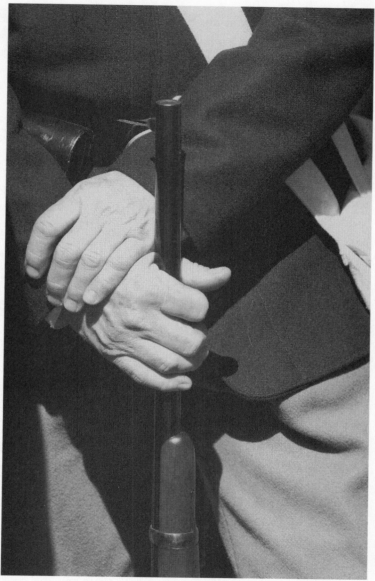

He had foolishly volunteered for a mission with which he believed he could earn a small sliver of revenge.

to climb through: Margaret was the only person at the school who could have convinced Ruby to treat him.

Ruby had been sent to work in the school by Margaret's father when he had learned the war had depleted most of its help. She had known Margaret her entire life. If Ruby had been asked to care for a wounded Rebel by anyone else she would have refused, but she cared about Margaret and was very loyal to her father. Without her healing skills, Isaac would have died in Sarah and Margaret's room in just a few hours.

But he didn't, and he spent the next few days in Sarah's bed, recovering.

And falling in love.

And he wasn't the only one.

*   *   *

It happened on Saturday morning.

The sun had just risen and the day's first light was peeking through the room's window. Sarah sat in a chair next to her bed caught between the twilight of sleep and consciousness. Isaac's eyes opened and took in the sight of his young protector. As they did, he was overcome with emotions he had never felt before. Tears started welling up in his eyes. For the first time in his life he felt as though there was someone out there who truly cared for him, even though he had done nothing to earn that kind of devotion. It was the greatest gift he had ever been given.

Sarah roused herself from her half-slumber and saw the tears on her wounded soldier's cheeks.

"What's wrong, Isaac?" she asked him. "Are you in a lot of pain?"

He shook his head. "No, I haven't felt this good in a long time."

"Then why are you crying?"

"Because you're here sitting beside me when I've known no one else in my life who would—"

"That can't be true."

"And not only are you the kindest and sweetest person I've ever known, you're also the prettiest."

Sarah blushed.

"So I was just laying here and I looked up at you and the tears just started coming and there wasn't anything I could do to stop them."

"That's so sweet." Sarah smiled.

"I love you, Sarah," he said quietly, afraid of how she would react to these powerful words.

Now it was Sarah's turn to cry. Tears came to her eyes as she bent over Isaac and gave him a long, deeply felt kiss on his lips. "I love you too, Isaac," she answered him.

"I love you both," a mumbled voice said from across the room, "but I'm trying to get some sleep, so could you keep the romantic declarations down a bit?"

"Sorry, Margaret," the two of them said together.

*   *   *

"I don't like the look of this leg," Ruby whispered to Sarah, so Isaac couldn't hear her. "I think the gangrene is starting to set in and there's not much more I can do. He's going to have to see a real doctor."

"And what would a doctor be able to do?" asked Sarah.

"Cut the leg off, I reckon," Ruby answered honestly. "Once the gangrene sets in, there's nothing else you can do."

"Are you sure?"

"I have heard tell that you can use maggots to eat away the dying flesh," Ruby admitted, "but I don't know where we could find as many as we would need, and he'd still lose his leg. I tell you now, Miss Sarah, if he stays here like this, he'll be dead in a few days."

"Then we'll have to get moving right away."

"We, Miss Sarah? Are you going to go with him?"

"Of course I am," Sarah answered her. "We're in love."

*   *   *

The secrecy of it all was too much of a burden for Ruby to carry. For almost a whole week she had managed not to tell anyone about the wounded soldier in Miss Sarah's bed, even though it had been extremely hard. But now, knowing that Miss Sarah was risking her own life to escape with the soldier, Ruby could no longer hold her tongue.

She told everything to Tulip, her partner in the kitchen, and she felt a great relief when the weight of the secret was lifted from her shoulders. Though she had bound Tulip to secrecy before telling her everything, the news of the wounded soldier soon spread throughout the college like a virus.

But it was too late. By the time the news reached the faculty, Sarah and Isaac were gone. Margaret refused to say when they left or where they were going. All she would admit was that she never expected to see her best friend ever again.

She never did.

*   *   *

"Sarah," Isaac groaned, "we *have* to stop."

"Just a bit further," she said.

"I can't take another step further!" He screamed in frustration, pushing himself out of Sarah's arms. He fell roughly to the ground, with tears streaming down his face. The pain was nothing like any he had ever experienced before. His whole leg felt like it was on fire—like his flesh was bubbling and melting off of his bones.

"We just have to get to the river," Sarah told him.

Isaac knew that there was a Confederate encampment on the other side of the Missouri River where he and Sarah would be safe at last, but the river was still four miles away and the thought of taking even one more step was too much for his mind to bear.

"It's no use. There's no way we can make it."

Sarah slapped him across the face. "Be a man!" she shouted. "It's just a few more miles! Once we get past the river, we're home free and the two of us can be together forever. Don't you want that?"

"Of course, I do."

"Then how can you sit there and give up?"

He shook his head. "You can't understand the pain I'm in."

"Is it worse than being dead? Tell me that! Because that's what you'll be if we stay here any longer. I know it hurts, but you have to ignore the pain and think of something much more important—the two of us together at the other side of that damn river!"

"Sarah, what has gotten into you?"

"We're just *so close*," she answered him. "We *can't* give up now!"

Isaac thought about this for a few precious moments before he gritted his teeth and stood back up. Sarah grabbed him and together they hobbled on.

*　　*　　*

Somehow they made it to the river, but now they had to cross it.

Last month's constant rainfall had caused the river to rise to the highest level it had been in decades. The water ran fast and was close to freezing. Every second in it was going to feel like the very worst kind of torture.

"We can do this," Sarah said.

"We're not going to make it," he answered realistically.

"We've come too far not to try. If we drown, at least we do it knowing that we got as close as this."

Isaac stared at her for a moment.

"How did I ever find you?" he asked her admiringly.

"You climbed in the right window," she answered him with a smile. "Now are you ready?"

"Yes," he nodded.

"Then let's go."

*　　*　　*

Their bodies were never recovered.

The icy water took them before they even got a quarter of the way across the river. As they went under, they held onto each other, both of them knowing that this would not be the end.

They were right. It wasn't.

*   *   *

Margaret was alone in her and Sarah's room. Even though it was dark and she was very tired, she could not sleep. The thought of her best friend and Isaac out there trying to survive in hostile territory was too powerful to allow her to sleep. Never a very religious person, she nevertheless found herself beginning to pray.

"Okay God, I don't ask for much, but please keep Sarah and Isaac safe."

"I'm afraid it's too late for that," a familiar voice answered her.

"Sarah?" Margaret sat up quickly in her bed, but she couldn't see her friend. As far as her eyes were concerned, she was still the only person in the room.

"We didn't make it, Margaret," the same familiar voice said.

"Sarah? Where are you? I can hear you, but I can't see you."

"There's nothing to see," the voice answered her. "Our bodies are at the bottom of the Missouri River.

"What are you saying?"

"We're dead, my friend. Isaac is here with me. He tried to say something, but you can't hear him, I guess."

"Why not?"

"I don't know," Sarah answered truthfully.

"Are you two in heaven?"

"I don't think so, unless heaven looks like our room."

"You mean you're actually in here, right now?"

"That's right. I just wanted to…" She continued speaking, but Margaret couldn't make out what she said.

"Your voice is fading away," she told her friend's spirit. There was no answer.

*   *   *

Margaret was expelled from the college for her role in the incident. Before she left the school forever, she bade farewell to her two friends, whom she knew were still in the room they had once shared together. Though there was no answer, she did feel herself overcome by a sudden sensation of peace and warmth. Sarah and Isaac had said goodbye to her in the only way they now could.

The room was taken over by a pair of new students who were not told of the dramatic events that had occurred within its walls. They complained that the room felt inexplicably chilly no matter how warm it was outside, as if something was deliberately trying to keep them out of it. They also said that sometimes late at night they heard what sounded like two people making love.

By All Appearances

Elizabeth Maher's sweetheart, Cameron, was about to leave their hometown of St. Joseph, Missouri, to go to an out-of-state college and she wanted to give him a keepsake that would always remind him of her. She decided to have her photograph taken and made an appointment at the studio on Third and Felix, where an old dress shop used to be. The cost for one photograph amounted to almost of all of her savings—it was 1883 and the process was still fairly new and quite expensive—but she believed the cost was worth it. Her picture would be with Cameron wherever he went as a constant reminder that she was waiting for him back home.

During the long walk from her parent's house to the studio, she got caught in a sudden breeze that blew off her hat and mussed up her hair. She prayed that she could fix it at the studio, not wanting to spend a small fortune on a photograph in which she didn't look perfect. Luckily the photographer had a small dressing room in his studio for exactly this situation and pointed her toward it. Much relieved, she opened the door to the room and walked in only to discover that the room was already occupied.

Sitting at the room's dressing table was an exquisitely beautiful woman, looking at herself in the mirror, dressed in a gray silk dress that appeared to be decades out of style. Elizabeth stood stunned for a moment, partly because she wasn't expecting anyone to be there but also because she had never seen a more glamorous, attractive woman in her entire life.

"I'm sorry," she said when she caught herself staring. "I didn't know someone was in here," she explained. She let herself out and she sat down on a nearby chair and waited for the room to become free.

She explained to the photographer when he noticed her sitting there, "I'm just waiting for your other customer to finish up in there."

"But you're the only person I have scheduled for today," he answered.

"Then who is the woman in there right now?" Elizabeth asked.

"You're the first person to come into the studio since I got here," he said with authority.

"But I swear there's someone in there," she said as she got up and opened the door to the room. "See for yourself."

The room was empty.

"I'm not crazy," she said defensively, even though the photographer had done nothing to suggest that she was. Elizabeth hesitantly stepped into the room and took a seat at the dressing table and fixed her hair. As she sat there she felt unbearably hungry, far hungrier than she had ever felt before. She thought she was going to faint, but she fought against it and stood up to regain her composure. Once she stepped away from the table the feeling vanished and she felt no different than she had before she entered the room, but she remained perplexed by what had happened.

The look of confusion on Elizabeth's face was captured forever in the photograph she gave to Cameron. He found it unsettling and deliberately "lost" the photograph the first chance he got, and without that reminder of his sweetheart's existence, he promptly fell in love with a girl who worked at his college's bookstore.

*   *   *

Marianne L'Ange was not a rebellious daughter by any stretch of the imagination. She was a good girl who loved both of her parents and wanted only to please them in any way that she could, but she was also a very romantic young woman who felt very deeply that there was nothing in this world as perfect and wonderful as love. She desperately wanted to experience love, but it had so far eluded her.

But this was not for lack of opportunity. Marianne was a woman with that rare kind of beauty that bore the touch of magic—it was so powerful that most people who saw her for the first time were dumbstruck by it and found themselves unable to move until their self-consciousness finally kicked in. Nearly every man she came across, young and old, single and married, made it clear with either subtle clues or brash declarations that they wanted to be with her—in every manner the phrase suggests.

She had long grown weary of all of this attention. She hated the way her beauty turned virtually every man she met into a fawning dog, performing for her every trick he could to earn her attention. She wanted desperately to meet a man who would treat her like a normal woman, not some divine goddess whose presence had to be constantly worshipped. For a long time she despaired that she would never meet such a man, but then, just a week before her 20th birthday, her brother brought home an old college friend of his named Luther Parsons.

Luther was the first man Marianne had met who possessed that same touch of magic. Women followed him everywhere he went and made fools out themselves just to catch his eye for a moment. But unlike Marianne, he used this power to his advantage. He had not worked a day in his life since he left school, choosing instead to earn a living by accepting "gifts" from any woman willing to pay for his attention. A cold, cynical man, he believed the notion of love was a frivolous concept held onto only by the most simple of minds, yet for which he was grateful since it was from the largesse of those simple-minded souls that he was able to live as well as he did.

But he was beginning to tire of the life of a gigolo and was looking to retire by marrying a woman wealthy enough to keep him comfortable for the rest of his life. He thought he had found her the day he met the stunningly beautiful sister of his old friend Robert L'Ange.

The L'Anges were descendents of a wealthy French aristocrat who managed to escape from Paris rather than face the guillotine during the Revolution. He found his way to the colonies and ended up settling in Missouri, where a series of fortunate investments made him even wealthier than he had been before. This good fortune stayed with the family in the intervening decades and as a result, Robert stood to inherit a lot of money upon his father's death.

During one drunken night at a local pub, however, Robert confessed to Luther that his wild ways had led him to contract both syphilis and tuberculosis. It was highly unlikely that he would live long enough to see any of his inheritance. Instead, the money would most likely go to his sister.

For Luther, the situation couldn't be any more ideal. By marrying Marianne he would not only stand to acquire a large fortune in the future, he would also earn the respect and admiration that would come with possessing the heart of one of the most beautiful women in the world. Many men had tried and failed, but he knew just how to take her—he would pretend she didn't exist.

Marianne—already drawn to his good looks—quickly became obsessed with him as soon as it appeared that he couldn't care less about impressing her. The more he ignored her the more obsessed she became, until finally he was all she thought about. She did everything she could to capture his attention, and on those rare occasions when she did, she felt a rush of excitement that she had never before experienced. Though he seemed to remain indifferent to her, she managed to spend more and more time with him, hoping that with each passing minute she could someday convince him that they were meant to be together.

Then one day her dream came true. She didn't see it coming. Completely out of the blue and without a single warning, he turned up at her home and asked her to marry him. She said yes without hesitation, afraid that a single pause might cause him to reconsider the question.

But there was a problem. Her parents did not approve of Luther and they forbade Marianne to marry him. And despite her instinct to always heed their wishes, she could not in this case. For the first time in her life, she rebelled against them and married Luther with neither their consent nor their knowledge.

The newlyweds moved to St. Joseph, where they lived in a hotel room on Third and Felix. It was the room he had used as a home base during his days as a gigolo, and he always paid for it several months in advance so that it was always available for him. They would be able to stay there for six months before the next payment was due.

They were happy at first. Marianne was overjoyed about spending time with the man that she loved and Luther enjoyed being intimate with someone he actually found attractive. But it did not last. He quickly grew bored of her company and began to regret the marriage when he realized that they could be together for years until she inherited the family fortune. Then it got worse.

A message arrived. It was from Marianne's parents. In the letter they made it clear that she was no longer a part of their family and would not be welcomed in their home ever again. Despite a lifetime spent honoring their every command, save one, Marianne would not be forgiven for her one act of rebellion. She would not inherit a cent from them, and any attempt by her to contact them would be ignored.

*   *   *

Dolly Harper needed a dress that would catch the eye of Winston Leroy when he saw her at the spring dance that Saturday night. She knew that Susan Montag was also looking to arouse the interest of St. Joseph's most eligible young bachelor, so it would have to be an extra special dress, and there was only one place in town where she could find such a dress—Lucretia Turner's dress shop on Third and Felix.

There she found just the dress that she had in mind. It was very expensive, but she truly believed it was worth every penny. The dress was a little long and required a bit of hemming, but Lucretia was happy to provide that for free. She asked Dolly to stand on a stool as she grabbed some pins and started marking the dress for alterations.

As Lucretia bent over to add another pin, Dolly screamed with fright. The sound was so sudden and shocking that Lucretia almost swallowed the pins she was holding between her teeth. She jumped up to see what was wrong and saw the hazy figure of a woman standing in the mirror in front of them. Hazy or not, Lucretia could see that the woman was very beautiful and dressed in a gray silk dress that hadn't been in style in years.

Dolly ran out of the store in the new dress, not even bothering to grab her own clothes. Lucretia soon followed her. Dolly never returned. Lucretia did, but only to pack up her goods and move them to another location. Not long after that, a photographer took over the space.

*   *   *

The letter from Marianne's parents threw Luther into a rage. His bet on her had just gone bust and he was a very sore loser. He used his fists to take out his frustrations and she was their unfortunate target. When he tired of beating her, he grabbed a suitcase and stuffed it with everything

The hazy figure of a woman was dressed in a gray silk dress that hadn't been in style in years.

valuable that they owned and walked out the door. She never saw him again.

All that she had left was her gray silk dress and the four months for which the hotel room was paid. She didn't know what to do. She could think of only one way she could earn the money she needed to live, but she could not bring herself to even consider it.

She tried to contact her family, but her brother was too ill to help her and all of her attempts to contact the rest of her family were ignored. Despite the hopelessness of her situation, her pride would not allow her to show any outward signs of how dire her life had become. She kept her dress immaculate and always looked perfect whenever she left her hotel room. No one who saw her had any idea that she was literally starving to death and didn't have a penny to her name.

The woman who lived in the next room found her. When she noticed that Marianne hadn't come out of her room for several days, she became concerned. She knocked on the door and when there was no response, she discovered it wasn't locked and let herself in. She found the poor, lifeless girl lying on the floor.

Marianne, the beautiful daughter of wealthy parents, had starved to death and was buried in an unmarked pauper's grave.

Her parents had thought they were doing the right thing when they turned their backs on her, but when they learned of her death they knew that they had been horribly wrong. Upon hearing the news, her father traveled to St. Joseph to exhume her body so it could be placed in the family mausoleum. While he was in town, he visited the hotel room where she died.

Standing in the room, he broke down and wept, unable to forgive himself for what he had allowed to happen. When the woman next door, who discovered Marianne's body, walked into the room to console him, she was shocked to see Marianne standing behind her weeping father.

Marianne's father noticed the look of horror and confusion on the woman's face and turned to see what had caused such a reaction. He fainted when he saw his daughter, standing in her gray silk dress, looking at herself in the room's one mirror. When he awoke, the spirit was gone.

From that day on, Marianne's spirit has been seen off and on in the building on Third and Felix throughout its many different incarnations. She always looks the same and she always appears in front of a mirror—making sure that she keeps up her appearance.

Jackson County Jail

The day John Hobbs found out that his wife, Moira, had left him for another man, even though he had long dreamed of the day he would be freed of the old ball and chain, his first reaction when it finally happened wasn't to shout out with joy but instead to cry in despair. Overcome with a sadness he didn't know he was capable of, he tried to fight it by consuming every last bit of alcohol he had. Consuming one very old bottle of wine and half a jug of bathtub gin, he quickly became very drunk, but when his sadness still refused to go away, he left the house and went out to find Independence, Missouri's most reliable moonshiner, Clayton Rohmer.

It was 1924 and Prohibition was still in effect, so John had little choice but to find Clayton if he wanted to continue drinking his sorrows away. Unfortunately for John, he ran into one of Independence's fine deputies on his way to the county's best source of bootleg liquor. He was arrested for public drunkenness and taken to the Jackson County Jail.

John had never been in the jail before, as he was by nature a decent and law-abiding fellow, but even in his drunken state, he was shocked to discover that it closely resembled the dungeons he had seen in several castles in Europe as a soldier in the First World War.

"This isn't an American jailhouse," he slurred angrily as he was led into his cell. "Whatcha gonna do? Put me in manacles? Torture me with burning hot pokers?"

The deputy just rolled his eyes and kept quiet as he shut the cell's door and locked the old drunk in for the night.

"Now settle down and get some sleep," he ordered John, who was too busy crying to hear him.

John had collapsed on the small cot in the cell and wept over his great misfortune. This lasted for 10 minutes before he passed out snoring. Chances are he would have stayed that way until morning, were it not for a chill that entered his body during the middle of the night. It woke him up so quickly and so powerfully that he shot up with a start, now completely sober and uncomfortably aware that he wasn't alone.

It had been a slow month at the jail, and only a third of its 12 cells were in use that night. The Deputy Marshall on duty was reading a new Sherlock Holmes story in *Colliers* to pass the time. Apart from the snores coming from the cell they had thrown the drunk into, it had been a very quiet night, so when the scream erupted from the drunk's cell, it nearly stopped the officer's heart. Taken by total surprise, he had to calm himself down for a minute before he was able to get up and investigate.

With his hand on his holstered gun, he carefully opened the cell's door. What he found nearly caused him to faint. There, sweating and bug-eyed on the cot was the drunk. His whole body was shivering as if he had been suddenly plunged into a tub of ice water, and his once-brown hair was now completely and inexplicably white.

The only thing that kept the deputy from passing out was the knowledge that this was not the first time this had happened in the Jackson County Jail, and it would most likely not be the last.

*   *   *

Many who enter the cell experience a sudden chill followed by a wave of stomach-churning nausea.

The Jackson County Jailhouse in Independence, Missouri, was built in 1859. Constructed out of limestone, its 12 cells were little more than dark, dank closets. Connected to the jailhouse was a home for the local Marshall and his family. It wasn't as nearly as depressing.

From the time it opened in 1860 through to 1933, it held thousands of prisoners, including such famous outlaws as Frank James and William Quantrill, but its most productive period came between the years 1861 and 1865, when the Civil War ensured that none of its cells ever went empty.

During that time the jail counted many women and children among its prisoners, most of them held there for giving aid to the state's anti-Union forces. At times the cells were filled beyond capacity and it wasn't uncommon for weaker prisoners to die within the jailhouse's walls. Missouri's divided loyalties during the war also helped to whittle down the jail's population, since it was common for supporters of both sides to share the same cell. The arguments that often resulted were sometimes fatal, and not just for the prisoners. The jail's first Marshall, Jim Knowles, was killed when he attempted to stop one of these passionate fights.

The other officer who died in the jailhouse was a young deputy who was murdered during an attempted jailbreak in 1866. Though his name has been lost to time, many have speculated that it is his spirit that haunts the prison. Others have argued that the ghost is Marshall Knowles, while some believe that there is not one spirit but many, all of them belonging to the women and children who were imprisoned—and sometimes died—in those dark, dank cells. A few people have even suggested that the jail is haunted by the ghost of its most famous outlaw, Frank James, but in all likelihood this is simply wishful thinking.

Encounters with these spirits are said to range from the horrific to the benign. Of all of them, the tale of what happened to poor John Hobbs is by far the worst. He never was able to tell anyone what he saw that night and he spent the rest of his life in a local asylum. The closest he ever came to describing what had happened to him in his cell was when he told a friend who had come to visit him that he had seen "a man in blue." But he never told anyone what this man in blue had done to frighten him to the point of insanity.

Many who enter the cell experience a sudden chill followed by a wave of stomach-churning nausea. There have also been reports of radios turning themselves on and off at random intervals and—most eerily—the sound of women and children crying late at night.

But none of these strange occurrences kept people out of the building after it closed over 70 years ago. Since then it has been completely restored and turned into a museum. Between March and October, tourists are welcome to tour both the jail and the adjoining house, and it isn't uncommon for these visitors to report feelings of anxiety and unease when they reach the cells. Many of these people have never heard the tales of the ghosts that are said to haunt the building, but they are seldom surprised when told about them once they've completed the tour. There is just something about the place that gets into people's bones and stays there until they can't take it anymore and have to leave.

Perhaps someday the folks who run the museum will finally learn the true identity of the spirit or spirits that haunt the old Jackson County Jailhouse, and discover just what John Hobbs meant when he described the man in blue. But on the chance that they never do, why don't you take a trip to Independence and visit the jail to see if you can find out the answer for yourself.

Who knows, you just might look really good with white hair.

Hannah's Horror

Hannah had been alone in her room studying for her upcoming French test when there was a knock on her door.

"Hannah?" a voice spoke as the door opened and a head poked through the doorway. It was Gladys, one of her sorority sisters. "You have a visitor waiting for you downstairs *and*," she whispered, "*he's really cute*."

"A visitor?" asked Hannah, the surprise in her voice bringing out her already very strong Polish accent. "Tell him I'll be right down," she said as she closed her book and checked her reflection in her mirror.

Gladys turned around and went downstairs to pass on Hannah's message while Hannah combed her hair and put on a touch of red lipstick. Unable to think of who her visitor could be, she walked tentatively out of her room and down to the house's front room, which was the only room in the sorority men were allowed to enter.

Her heart almost leapt out of her chest when she saw Josef Steinberg sitting uncomfortably on the sorority's frilly white love seat.

"Hannah!" he shouted when he saw her. He jumped up with open arms and she eagerly greeted him with a hug.

"Josef," she said with disbelief, speaking in their mother tongue. "I can't believe it is you."

Hannah and Josef had grown up together in a small farming village just outside of Warsaw. Though they were not related, their families had been so close that the two considered each other like brother and sister.

"You have grown up so much, Hannah," he compli-mented her. "You have become a very beautiful woman. Just like your mother."

The mention of her mother brought tears to Hannah's eyes. She had not heard from her family in over a year, since the day of the Nazi invasion.

"Have you seen them, Josef?" she asked. "Have you any word from my parents?"

Her heart broke when she saw Joseph trying to hold back his tears. At once she knew he was there to deliver the worst of all possible news. It was now simply a matter of her hearing it.

"They are gone," he cried. "Your family, my family, they are all gone. We are the only two who are left."

Hannah went numb. She did not cry or scream or do any of the things she so desperately wanted to. She just stood there, unable to imagine a world in which her fam-ily did not exist.

"What happened?" she said in a voice barely above a whisper.

"They herded them like cattle into railway cars and took them to a camp in Auschwitz. They said it was just so that they could be relocated to a new ghetto, but it was all a lie. I was in England at the time, at art school—"

"You were always such a good artist," Hannah added awkwardly.

"Thank you," he said sadly. "Were I not, I would have been on the train with them. A friend of mine, he was not so lucky. He told me that the journey on the train was so horrible that some people died from the strain of it before they got to the camp. Once there they separated the men from the women and children, the young from the old. He watched as our families were sent to what they were told was a shower, but it was another lie."

The thought of what happened next caused Josef to burst out into a horrible sob. He collapsed on the love seat and wept loudly. Some of the girls in the building poked their heads through the front room's doorway to see what was happening, but no one interrupted the two of them.

Hannah forced herself to say, "Josef, what happened next?"

"They killed them. They killed them all and burned their bodies, but not before checking their teeth for gold fillings. My friend, he was forced to help those Nazi monsters carry the bodies out of the chambers and put them into the ovens. That was how he survived. He did this for two weeks before…he would not tell me how… I do not think *he could* tell me how…he escaped. By a series of miracles he found his way to me and told me what happened. As soon as he did I sold all of my art supplies and took all the money I saved and bought a ticket to America. It took me a long time to get to this place they call Missouri, but I made it. I had to come and tell you what had happened."

"But Josef, you could have…you could have sent a telegram."

He shook his head. "My friend, he risked his life to get to England to tell me what had happened to my family. It would be an insult to him if I did not do the same for you."

Hannah was still too numb to say anything else. Instead, she just held onto her friend and thought of the past that had led to this horrible moment.

Hannah was lucky enough to attend Columbia's University of Missouri.

Hannah had not wanted to leave. Her father had a brother who had traveled to America when he was just a small boy. His brother had come to the United States with nothing, but he worked hard and made many smart decisions and became a wealthy man. He lived in Columbia, Missouri, where he owned a dry goods store and a hotel. Thanks to his property and other investments, he was able to return back to the place of his birth and reunite with the family he had not seen in 30 years. It was then that he met Hannah, who amazed him with both her great beauty and intellect. He was so impressed by her that he suggested to her father that it would be in her best interest to return with him to America, where she could go to school at Columbia's University of Missouri. Only 17, and never having spent a single day away from her home, Hannah had no desire to leave her family, but her father insisted. It was a tremendous opportunity and he knew enough to know that life in Poland was soon going to become very difficult.

A very fast learner, Hannah quickly made the adjustment to the new language and found life at the university very exciting. At first she lived with her uncle, who was a bachelor, in the hotel that he owned, but six months into her stay he took ill with a terminal form of cancer. Before he died he attempted to get the rest of his family to America, but to no avail. He left his estate to Hannah in a trust that gave her an allowance until the completion of her education. After that, she would be free to do with it whatever she wished. She had moved out of the hotel and into the school's Jewish sorority, where she studied hard and did everything she could to try and contact her family.

"What are you going to do now?" she asked Josef as she embraced him. "Now that you have told me?"

"I don't know," Josef admitted. "I suppose I will find a job here in America. Is this Columbia a nice place to live? Maybe I shall stay here."

"What about your education?" she asked. "What about your art?"

"I have other concerns right now," he told her.

"But you are so talented."

"Talent means nothing if you starve to death," he said sadly.

"Wait here," Hannah said.

"Where are you going?"

"To my room. I shall just be a moment."

Hannah ran to her room and found her purse. In it she found $50, all that she had left from that month's allowance. She then went back downstairs and made a phone call before she returned to her friend in the front room.

Josef shook his head when she handed the money over to him. "I can not take this."

"You have to."

Josef looked at her and realized that it would be pointless to argue. He took the money.

"I want you to use it for food and art supplies," she said.

"What about shelter?" he asked. "Should I paint out on the street?"

"You have a room at the nearest hotel. For as long as you need it."

"How—" he started to ask.

"I own it," she explained. She went on when she realized that the first answer would inevitably lead to more questions. "My uncle left it to me. All you have to do is promise me that you will someday become a great artist."

"Hannah..."

"Promise me," she insisted.

"I will, Hannah," he promised. "I will for you."

"Good." She smiled as tears trickled down her cheeks. The enormity of what she had lost— her entire family— finally hit her, and she trembled and wailed almost uncontrollably in Josef's arms.

The sound of her cries again aroused the curiosity of her sorority sisters, and this time they could not stop themselves from finding out what was wrong. It was Gladys who asked Josef, as Hannah wept in his arms, what had happened.

Josef's English was not as good as Hannah's, even though he had spoken it for longer than she had, but Gladys understood him perfectly when he answered her.

"They're gone," he explained. "Her family is all gone."

When it become clear that Hannah was no longer consolable, Gladys and two other sorority sisters took her to her room. Josef left the house and did what Hannah asked; he bought some food, a drawing pad and some pencils and went to the nearest hotel where he had a room waiting for him.

Hannah had stopped crying but now was almost in a state of catatonia. Her sorority sisters decided that it would be best to just leave her alone so she could get some rest. Hannah lay quietly on her bed until she was sure she was alone. Then she sat up and walked over to her desk to compose a short letter. When she finished it, she stripped her sheets off of her bed and began to tear them into long strips. One by one, she tied each piece together to form a makeshift rope. She then tied one end of her improvised rope to her room's radiator and the other around her neck.

She did not even pause to contemplate the consequences of her actions. Instead, she just opened her window and climbed out of it. The sheet almost ripped apart from the strain, but it did its job. It snapped her neck in two and ended her pain forever.

Gladys discovered Hannah's body when she went to check on her friend. The sight of the taut handmade rope led her to the window and she screamed when she saw Hannah's dead, broken body hanging on the side of the house.

When the authorities arrived, Gladys showed them the note that Hannah had left on her desk. It read:

To Everyone,

There is no point to any of this anymore. I can think of no reason to continue living, so I have decided to end my life. I ask that the money and properties that are now in my name be given to Josef Steinberg, so that he can sell them and use the money to finance his career as an artist.

Hannah Landmann

Even though the note was not considered a legally binding will, there was no one to contest Hannah's wishes and her fortune was turned over to an extremely distraught Josef. He considered the money to be tainted and gave it away to an organization that helped Jewish families out of worn-torn Europe. He gave up the idea of being an artist and worked a series of menial jobs around Missouri before he died at the age of 27 in an industrial accident.

*   *   *

Not long after Hannah's suicide, her sorority moved out of the house in which it had long resided. It held too many bad memories, which they felt could not be forgotten with time. The house sat vacant for awhile before it was purchased by the Sigma Phi Epsilon Fraternity to serve as their new headquarters. The first person to live in Hannah's former room was a young man named Tom Schuman.

From the moment he entered the room he could tell that there was something wrong with it, but he didn't know what it could be. Neither he nor any of his fraternity brothers knew about Hannah or how she had died, so— for a time—they had no explanation for the odd things that happened in that room.

Tom's first clue that his unease about the room was warranted came one night when he was awakened by the sound of a young woman crying. At first he thought it might be coming from another room, but when he sat up in his bed, he could tell that the crying was very close to him. He turned on the lamp next to his bed and found that he was alone, but the crying did not stop. He checked his closet—the only place a person could hide in the room—and saw that it was empty. It was only when he closed his closet door that the crying finally stopped. The next morning he asked the other fellows who lived on the third floor if they had heard the sound as well, but no one else had.

After this strange incident, other members of the fraternity began to see a strange, glowing red aura floating at the top of the third floor stairway. Eventually, after several more bizarre experiences like this, the Sigma Eps learned about Hannah and the room where she had ended her own life.

Though plans to remodel the third floor had already been underway at that point, it became even more of a priority once they knew that one of its rooms had once housed a suicide. The room where Hannah died no longer exists, but her spirit continued to haunt the building anyway.

After the remodeling, members of the fraternity returned from Christmas holidays to discover that doors and windows, which had been firmly locked and shut, were now all wide open, yet nothing inside the house was missing or stolen. It led many to believe that the incident was not the result of a normal breaking and entering.

One fraternity member named Mark Merlotti insisted that he saw Hannah's spirit reflected in a mirror one night while he was studying in his room. He saw the reflection out of the corner of his eye, but when he turned to get a better look at it, it vanished. Another Sigma Ep, Ray Lorenz, told a local paper that he was awakened one night by the sight of a young woman "who looked like she was made out of ivory" walking toward his bed.

Despite these many different occurences, no one has ever figured out what keeps Hannah's ghost attached to the building where she died. Is it a punishment for the rashness of her actions? Or an inability to move on? Whatever the reason, it is nothing less than tragic. By remaining at the Sigma Phi Epsilon fraternity, Hannah's spirit is denying itself something it must long for more than anything else: to be reunited with the family whose horrific deaths led her to take her life in the first place.

3
Sightings Along the Way

The Pedestrian

Since the days of the Model T Ford, many a traveler along the roads of Kansas City, Missouri, has been saved by the helpful spirit of Frank Louter as he walks the streets warning drivers of the potential dangers that lurk ahead. He has been on the job for over 80 years; his story starts in 1922 when Frank was having some trouble dealing with his rebellious son, Charlie.

Charlie was the kind of teenager who believed he had all the answers and was too old to be beholden to his father's rules. To flaunt his newfound independence he had taken to hanging out with a group of local delinquents who specialized in vandalism and petty thievery. Frank had ordered his son to stay away from these bad influences, but Charlie ignored his father's wishes and continued to hang out with them whenever he could.

One evening, Frank stopped Charlie as the boy was about to leave the house. "Where do you think you're going?"

"Out," his son answered sharply.

"And where is that?"

"Right around none of your business!"

"Watch your mouth, young man!" advised Frank.

"Or what?"

"You really don't want to find out the answer to that question," answered Frank.

"Or maybe it's just a hollow threat you can't back up," said Charlie, which was a pretty accurate interpretation of Frank's statement. "Now get out of my way!"

"You're not going anywhere."

"Who's going to stop me?"

"Who do you think?" Frank said as he crossed his arms in front of his chest. Charlie may have been 17 and fully grown, but he knew he was still no match for his father. So instead of fighting his dad, he screamed out with frustration, turned around and went to his room.

Frank felt good, having stopped his son from doing something stupid for at least one night. Unfortunately, he had—like so many parents before and after him—failed to consider how easy it would be for his son to simply slip out of his bedroom window, which is exactly what Charlie did.

That night, Charlie's friends had managed to steal a couple of bottles of moonshine from a local bootlegger. Prohibition had been in effect since Charlie was 14, so he had never had a chance to taste alcohol before. It was hard for him to understand its appeal because what he drank tasted a lot like gasoline, only with a more unpleasant aftertaste. But he didn't want his friends to think he was a sissy, so he equaled their intake, swallow for swallow. It didn't take long before he was staggeringly drunk, a condition that his friends also fell victim to.

Out of booze and bored with their present location, the eight boys decided to go for a ride. The car belonged to the father of one of Charlie's friends and was never meant to accommodate so many people, but they refused to be deterred. They all squeezed themselves inside the car, with the son of the car's true owner behind the wheel. He didn't really know how to drive, but at that point he was so drunk it wouldn't have really mattered if he did.

And to add to the overall danger quotient of their foolishness, a heavy fog began to roll out onto the road, making it almost impossible for anyone to see just a few feet ahead of them.

It was a minor miracle that they got as far as they did before the driver lost control of the vehicle and slammed into the side of a bridge. A couple that lived near the bridge heard the crash and alerted the authorities. The eight boys were taken to the nearest hospital, but only two of them were alive by the time they got there. Charlie was one of these two lucky survivors.

Frank was awakened by the sound of knocking on his front door. It was the police, there to inform him of his son's accident. Frank rushed to the hospital and found Charlie, drunk and inconsolable in an emergency room bed. Both of his legs were broken, but he was otherwise unscathed from the accident that had claimed the lives of six of his friends. As slurred as his words were, both from the alcohol and the pain, Frank still understood his son when he begged him for forgiveness.

"I never should have gone out like that," Charlie sobbed.

Frank forgave his son and told him that everything was going to be okay. "Everyone needs to have an experience that teaches them this lesson, and I'm sorry that it took the death of your friends for you to have yours," he said.

"I'm never drinking again," Charlie insisted. "And I'm never ever going to lie or steal or do anything wrong ever again."

"Easier said than done, Charlie. But as long as you try to live a good life, you should end up being as happy as you deserve."

Charlie eventually fell asleep, and Frank sat by his side until the morning. He spoke to his son's doctor and learned that Charlie was going to make a full recovery, so he decided to go back home and get some rest.

Having been up all night, Frank found it hard to keep his eyes open as he left the hospital. He yawned and stretched out his arms, which shielded his eyes from the bright morning sun. It was owing to his exhaustion and his upraised arm that he did not see the car driving toward him as he crossed the road. By the time he heard the car's horn, it was too late. He stood there helplessly as the vehicle drove right into him.

He was rushed right back into the hospital, but his injuries were too severe. He died within minutes of being hit. Charlie was awake when they brought his father in and he heard everything as the doctors labored unsuccessfully to save Frank's life. When he was told that his father was dead, he became consumed with guilt and sadness. As soon as his injuries healed, he disappeared from Kansas City and was never seen again.

The same could not be said for his dead father.

Eight years after his unexpected demise, the spirit of Frank Louter was first spotted and recognized by a veteran police officer who had been on the scene the morning when Frank was run over. He was in his car, driving during a day as foggy as the one on which Charlie's accident occurred, when he saw a solitary figure standing on the side of the road, waving him over. He stopped to see

On foggy mornings, a solitary figure can be seen standing on the side of the road.

what the person wanted, and did a double take when he recognized the long-deceased Louter. He closed his eyes and gave them a good rub and when he opened them again, the man was gone.

The experience spooked him enough that he had to sit for a minute before he felt ready to continue driving, but before he could, he heard the sound of a large crash in front of him. Reacting quickly, he raced toward the sound and found that two cars had collided in a freak accident. He jumped out of his vehicle to investigate and discovered that the crash had taken the lives of both drivers. A sudden shudder rose up the officer's spine when it occurred to him that had he not stopped at the beckoning of the ghostly figure, there was a good chance he would have been involved in the deadly accident. Frank had saved his life.

For more than 70 years since this first sighting, other motorists driving along the roads of Kansas City have claimed to avoid similar close calls thanks to the vigilant efforts of the city's protective pedestrian, whose good work serves as proof that some people, even in death, choose to turn tragedy into something much more beneficial.

The Phantom Rider

Anson Locke was lost. He could tell that his horses were getting jittery in the cold night air as they pulled him down a deserted country road. He suspected that he had to be somewhere near the small town of Sand Springs, but he couldn't be sure. The problem was that it was too dark. If the sun was out he could spot Roubidoux Creek and know exactly where he was, but it was so dark that he could barely see the backsides of his horses, even with his small lantern burning beside him.

He started to think that it might be a good idea to just stop for the night and wait for dawn, when his horses made his decision for him. They stopped without warning and nearly caused him to fall off his seat on the wagon. He tried to get them moving again, but it was clear that something had spooked them and they weren't going to budge.

I guess that's it then, he thought to himself. Luckily he kept a blanket in the back of the wagon for just this situation, so he found it and decided to get some sleep. It was quite chilly out, but it wasn't raining so he was unconscious in a matter of minutes. As he slept, his snores echoed throughout the countryside and his horses were getting more and more nervous.

"WHHHHHHHEEEEEEEEEEEEHHHHHH-HEEEEENNNNYYYAAAAAAA!"

The sound of his horses' cries awoke Anson with a start. Rubbing the sleep out of his eyes he sat up just in time to see a blazing light heading toward his wagon. Before he could move, his horses started running into the darkness away from the fiery presence approaching them in the distance. He was nearly thrown to the ground, but he managed to keep his balance and grab the reins before his team went out of control. There was nothing he could do to get them to stop or even slow down; his only option was to hold on and ride it out until they grew tired or something stopped them.

As he rode he continued looking back to catch glimpses of the strange light behind them, and with each glance he saw the light getting closer and closer to the wagon. Within a few minutes he could see that the light was coming from a rider on a horse. At first he assumed the rider was holding a lantern, but then he realized that the light was actually emanating from the rider and the horse together. They glowed like rays from the sun, and it was at that point that Anson became acutely aware that they were not of this world.

"Heeeyyyyyaaaaaaaa!" he shouted at his team, trying to get them to gallop even faster than they had been before, but they were already moving at top speed. He turned around and saw that the phantom rider was now just behind him. Never a religious man, Anson started to pray.

The luminescent team of man and horse began to overtake the wagon. Anson turned and got a good glimpse into the rider's eyes, which burned like embers. The phantom horse snorted loudly enough that the sound could be mistaken for thunder as it galloped ahead of the wagon and past his team.

Seeing that what they had been running from was now in front of them, his horses nearly killed themselves coming to a sudden stop. This time Anson wasn't able to stay in his seat and was catapulted off the wagon onto some soft, dewy grass below. Though the impact left him with a very large, black bruise, he was able to get up and return to the wagon without any broken bones or serious injuries.

Shaken from the incident, he decided to once again wait until dawn before going any further. Too nervous to sleep, he sat in the back of the wagon and tried to convince himself that there must be a rational explanation for what had just happened to him. All rational thought vanished, however, when he saw another light appear in the darkness behind the wagon. His heart nearly leapt out of his chest when he realized that this time there was more than one light. There looked to be about a dozen!

He grabbed the horses' reins as quickly as he could and tried to get them moving, but they would not budge. "Come on!" he shouted at them. "You couldn't run fast enough before!" It was no use. They weren't going anywhere.

Not knowing what else to do he jumped into the back of the wagon and underneath the blanket. He could hear the sound of a dozen horses approaching him and he began to shake uncontrollably from the thought of having 12 burning sets of eyes staring down at him.

"I think there's someone in there," he heard a voice say after the sound of galloping hooves had stopped.

"Sure is," another voice agreed. "I can see him shivering underneath that blanket."

Anson screamed when he felt the blanket being ripped off of him. He covered his face and hoped that whatever they did to him, they did it quickly.

"His eyes glowed red and they looked straight down into my soul!"

"Aw, quit your screaming," he heard someone say. "We're not going to hurt you."

Anson slowly took his hands away from his face and saw that he was surrounded by a dozen normal-looking men on horses, each one with a lamp in his hand.

"I take it you've seen what we've been chasing all night," one of them said to him. Anson could tell by the way the man looked that he was the leader of the group.

"His eyes glowed red," Anson blurted out, "and they looked straight down into my soul!"

"That's our fellow, all right," the man said. "Did you happen to see which way he went?"

"That way." Anson pointed straight ahead. "You're not going to go after him, are you?"

"We're going to try, but if tonight is anything like every other night we've tried to catch this spook he's long gone by now."

"What is he?"

"Best we can tell," the man answered, "he's a fellow who isn't very happy to be dead. His name's Charles Potter and he's been riding these roads for going on 20 years now."

"A ghost? You're trying to catch a ghost? Can you even do that?"

"Well, we haven't yet," the man said, "but that doesn't mean it isn't in our best interests to try."

"But why?"

"Because it isn't much fun for the locals around here to be terrorized by him whenever they're out on the road at night and because—" The man paused to reflect for a moment and continued. "Because he died trying to do a good thing, so it's wrong for his soul to remain here on Earth when it should be getting its just rewards. From what my father told me, he would have done the same for any one of us."

With that the man nodded at Anson and started galloping away toward the ghost. The rest of his men followed and Anson was left alone with his wagon. Barely able to comprehend what had just happened to him, he looked to the sky and saw—much to his great relief—that the sun was beginning to rise.

*　　　*　　　*

Elder Maupins was a very complex man. Unlike so many of his contemporaries he was not content to choose one career with which to define himself—that was a path followed by lesser mortals, those who had never been graced with the good Lord's blessings. No, Elder used the gifts God had given him to pursue two very different vocations. By day he was Preacher Maupins, head of Sand Springs, Missouri's tiny nondenominational church, and by night he was the leader of the Maupins Raiders, a vicious gang that terrorized the people of Pulaski County and anyone unlucky enough to run into them.

People may wonder how a man could justify being both a man of the cloth and the leader of a violent criminal gang, and the answer to that question is surprisingly simple. Elder could justify his seemingly antithetical occupations because he was completely insane. No one knew exactly when it was that he lost his mind—or if he had ever even fully possessed it to begin with—but it was clear to everyone that he saw no contradiction between praising the Lord by day and robbing and killing the Lord's children by night.

Over the years people tried to stop his reign of terror, but everyone who did met an unfortunate end. Soon there was no one in the county brave enough to stand up to Elder and his gang; even the sheriff decided long ago it was in his best interest to turn a blind eye to the raiders' nefarious exploits. For a time it seemed as though the county would never be free from the hold of Maupins' insanity, until a former Rebel soldier moved to Sand Springs and decided it was time to take a stand.

Charles Potter had lost everything he had during the war. While he was off fighting for the Rebel army, his wife was executed by Union troops for her work in the Confederate underground. They burned his house to the ground and sent his 13-year-old son to the local jailhouse, where he caught ill with a fever and died. Charles didn't know any of this until after the war had ended and he returned home to discover that it wasn't there. For a time he considered ending his own life, but that was the way of a coward and he would sooner live with his misery forever than bring the shame of such ignominy to his name.

Instead he traveled in search of a place to start a new life. For reasons he himself never understood he ended up settling in Sand Springs, and once there it didn't take him long to find out about the insane preacher whose cruelty kept the town in a constant state of fear. As much as he hated cowards, Charles hated bullies even more. That was why he joined the Confederate army in the first place.

By nature a peaceful man who was very much against the concept of slavery, he could not stomach the government's efforts to force the states to bow to its will, so he chose to fight for a side whose beliefs he did not completely share. It didn't take him long before he grew disgusted by the situation in his newly adopted home. All around him there were cowards—too cowed by fear to defend themselves—and the bullies who used that fear to take whatever they wanted. It was time, he decided, for someone to take a stand.

Early one Sunday morning in the last month of 1865, Charles got dressed in his Confederate uniform, saddled up his horse, Violet, and set out on the most important ride of his life.

Elder Maupins was standing in front of his flock that morning warning them of the dangers of sin. It was the same sermon he gave every Sunday—the only one he knew—and the only thing that kept the frightened people in the small church's pews from staying home was the fear of what would happen if they did. It was better, they believed, to humor Maupins' delusions than to risk displeasing him with their absence.

He was just about to start the part of his oratory where he began to shout at the Devil and urge the fallen angel to appear so he could beat him back down to hell with his bare hands, when the door to the church burst open and a man on a horse rode in toward the demented preacher. In the man's hand was a sword, which he brandished in the air, ready to use it to strike down the man who had tormented the county for far too long, but before he could a shot rang out inside the church. The rider cried out in pain and fell to the ground. His horse reared up on its hind legs and turned around and ran off. The man bled to death inside the church. No one knew where the shot had come from.

Many believed that this would deter anyone from ever again attempting to stop Maupins, but what they didn't know was just how determined Charles Potter was to complete his mission. He wasn't about to let something as insignificant as his own death stop him from chasing the mad preacher out of Sand Springs forever.

Two months after his death, the local blacksmith reported seeing a strange glowing figure ride past him on one of the local roads. A month later the glowing rider was seen by all four members of a local family. Three months after that a traveling salesman reported seeing the same sight, and after that stories of people encountering this phantom rider became so frequent that no one bothered to keep track of them.

But somehow, despite how widespread the news of this phantom horseman was around the county, it never reached the ears of Preacher Maupins. He was too busy tending to the demands of his own insanity to pay attention to the local Sand Springs gossip. In the end, he must have wished he had.

It was a cold October night when he and his fellow marauders were on their way to a farm whose owner was late in paying the tribute they had demanded for not breaking his legs and stealing everything he owned. Though the air was calm when they set out on the road, dark clouds quickly gathered above them and they were hit by a powerful storm. By then they were too far from their base of operations to turn back, so they continued on to the farm. And as they rode they saw something that appeared to be a beacon in the distance.

"What could that be?" asked Teddy Jergans, Maupins' second-in-command.

"It's a light," answered Maupins.

"I know that, but where is it coming from?"

"Don't you know?" asked Maupins.

"Would I have asked you if I did?"

"It's the Lord's light guiding us to our duty."

"The Lord wants us to beat and maim a farmer and steal everything he owns?"

"I am not here to question his desires, only to make sure that they are acted out."

Teddy shook his head. Sometimes his boss was too crazy for even him to take. If it weren't for all of the money and violence, he would have left Maupins' gang years ago.

Maupins turned and shouted to the rest of his men. "Let us ride toward God's light so we can mete out his infinite justice without any haste!" By now they were all so used to his craziness that they just stayed quiet and followed him as he began to ride toward the beacon at a full gallop.

Lightening began to flash around them, quickly followed by the roars of thunder, but Maupins refused to be deterred by nature's wrath and considered these forces of nature to be proof that he was doing exactly what his Lord wanted him to. He dug his spurs deeply into his horse's sides, even though the poor creature was already racing as fast as it could go.

The gang moved closer and closer to the light, but the rain made it impossible for them to see its true source even as they were almost upon it.

"Faster! Faster!" Maupins shouted as they came to within a quarter of a mile of the beacon. The light grew larger with each step, but still they could not see its source.

And then it disappeared.

"Lord, is this a sign?" Maupins shouted out to the sky as he brought his exhausted horse to a stop. "Why did you extinguish that which you wanted us to follow?"

As if to answer him, the rain suddenly stopped, leaving the marauders with a clear view of the road around them. There was nothing there except the men and their horses.

Teddy recognized the area they were in and realized it was nowhere near the farmhouse. "It appears that the Lord wanted us to be in the middle of nowhere," he mumbled under his breath. Unfortunately, his words were clear enough to reach Maupins' ears.

"Blasphemer!" Maupins shouted as he slapped Teddy in the mouth. The blow was so powerful that it knocked him off of his horse. He fell to the wet ground with a muddy splat.

"You crazy, no-good—" Teddy cussed as he lifted himself off of the ground. He was interrupted by the sound of a bullet whizzing past his ear.

"I have no use for your kind in my midst," Maupins said to him with a smoking revolver in his right hand.

Teddy froze where he stood as he tried to decide what to do next. If he tried to reach for his revolver, Maupins would be sure to shoot him down. If he tried to run,

Maupins could shoot him in the back. His only hope was to convince the madman that it didn't make any sense to kill him.

"I'm sorry, Preacher," he apologized. "I don't know what came over me. Did I say something to offend the Lord's ears?"

"You're a devil, Jergens. I should have known it all along. You have been sent to me to spy on the Lord for your master, Lucifer!"

"That's not true, Preacher," Teddy insisted.

"Liar! You will say anything to protect your fallen master!"

"Aw, heck." Teddy knew now that he had no other option but to make a miracle play for his sidearm. Tensing his body, he whipped his hand down to his holstered weapon. As his hand gripped his revolver's handle, his eyes blinked and during that millisecond a powerful explosion rocketed him off his feet.

On his back he used his hands to search for the bullet wound and realized that he was uninjured. He opened his eyes and saw a large smoking crater just a few feet from the spot where he had been standing. He heard the sound of rapid hoof steps and turned to see all the raiders galloping away down the road. He sat up and saw that there were only two people left with him. One was Maupins, who was on his knees, and the other was a familiar looking man on a horse, who was glowing.

"I am here as your humble servant, my Lord." Maupins prayed to the glowing rider. "I have dedicated my life to serving your will and I thank you for finally recognizing my work by appearing in front of me on this glorious night!"

Teddy couldn't believe that Maupins actually believed that the phantom rider was actually God when it was obvious to him that it was the fool he had shot in the church last December. He briefly considered sharing this information with Maupins, but he remembered what the preacher was about to do to him before the lightning bolt had knocked him to the ground. He decided to let the crazy man sort this mess out for himself.

Maupins continued to praise the glowing figure in front of him. Even as the rider pulled out a sword from its scabbard, he did not waver in his devotion. He kept on praying to it right until the second the phantom rider cut off his head.

Teddy screamed at the sight of Maupins' head falling to ground, and he screamed even louder when it started rolling near his feet. He screamed the loudest when he saw the horseman ride toward him and then—following the sound of a sword slicing its way through meat and bone— his screaming stopped.

*   *   *

Many posses tried to capture the phantom rider over the following years, but none of them ever came close. Eventually, though, sightings of him riding along the roads of Roubidoux County grew fewer and fewer, until finally—around the end of the Great Depression—they stopped for good.

The ghost of Elder Maupins on the other hand…well…that's another story altogether.

The Hermit of Knob Noster

There are many reasons why people choose to remove themselves from the outside world. For some it is fear; for others, disdain. Some do so because they have been wronged and never wish to be again, while others do so because they have wronged and do not wish to be found. Whatever the reason, society has bestowed a special name to all those who have decided to shun the company of their fellow men: hermit.

It is a word that arouses many different feelings—sadness, pity, fear and curiosity being the most common. The paradox of becoming a hermit is that by removing yourself from society, those who know of your existence will only become more curious about who you are and why you have made this extreme decision. If you are really good at being one and actually manage to avoid being seen, you will become the subject of much rumor and speculation, all of which will inevitably lead to tales of past crimes or current misdeeds. Though you may be innocent of any societal transgressions, your behavior will make you suspect and people will come to assume the very worst of you.

This was how it was for the stranger who lived outside of the town of Knob Noster, just a few years after the country had won the Revolutionary War. No one knew his name or where he was from, and his only companion was a slave who answered to the name of Daniel. Daniel was a friendly fellow, well liked by everyone who came his way,

He was perfectly entitled to keep his privacy if that was what he wanted.

much to the surprise of those rare few to had ever had contact with his master.

The unfriendly stranger almost never ventured into the town, but when he did his appearance was so unsettling that people would run inside their homes rather than encounter him on the street. He was a very tall man, thin and gaunt, with a long hooked nose and yellow teeth. His long, greasy black hair hung over his eyes, and his left eye was blinded with an ugly cataract. He walked with a hunch, though this was more out of poor posture than a curve of his spine, and he smelled very, very bad. It was a scent that clearly indicated that neither his skin nor his clothes had been washed in a very long time.

He only came into town to purchase supplies such as flour or coffee. People wondered how this man, who had no apparent means, got the money necessary to purchase these goods and how he had come to own a slave. Some suggested he was an outlaw who had retired after a life spent as a highwayman. Others decided that he had been the son of a wealthy family who had murdered his relatives and taken his fortune with him to his shack outside of town. Then there were those who speculated that he had come across a long-lost chest of buried treasure.

Some of the locals felt that the sheriff of Knob Noster was duty bound to learn the truth of the stranger's mysterious wealth, but, as far as he was concerned, there was no evidence that the hermit had done anything wrong and he was perfectly entitled to keep his privacy if that was what he wanted. Occasionally, after a night of drinking, some of the local men would devise plans to visit the stranger and discover the true source of his wealth, but the memory of his intimidating presence was always enough to make them reconsider.

This was how it was for several years, but things started to change when people noticed that they never saw Daniel around town anymore. In the past he had come into Knob Noster at least once or twice a week, but it had been months since anyone had seen him last. It didn't take long for suspicion to mount. Everyone believed that the genial slave had met an untimely end at his master's hands. Once again the sheriff was urged to investigate, but without any evidence of a crime having been committed, he could make only the most cursory of inquiries.

It didn't help the stranger's case when he started showing up in town much more frequently than he ever had before. No one accused him directly of being a murderer, but that was only because there was no one in Knob Noster who was willing to speak with him.

Several more years passed, but little changed when it came to how the townspeople treated the stranger. One little boy claimed that the man had once tried to speak to him but he ran off home to his mother before he could hear what the man said. Most assumed the boy was lying, and it was generally accepted that the stranger had not spoken to another soul since the disappearance of Daniel.

It had been five years since then, and the following summer proved to be as hot and cruel as anyone in Knob Noster could recall. Weeks passed without rain and the earth turned to dust from the drought, so no one, of course, was annoyed when storm clouds suddenly filled the sky. At last it was going to rain! Their relief, however, was short lived when the storm that erupted was the most destructive and violent of any they had ever seen.

They sat at their windows and watched as the lightning flashed and the thunder roared, thankful that none of them were unfortunate enough to be caught in the middle of this tumultuous downpour. And as they sat there, they began to see a light flicker in the distance. It appeared to be the glow of a lantern swaying back and forth in the wind. To everyone's horror it appeared that some poor soul *was* caught outside in the storm and was desperately attempting to reach the shelter the town provided. Their fears were confirmed when a flash of lightning lit up the sky behind the lantern's glow and gave everyone a glimpse of the unfortunate figure. It was the hermit.

Had it been anyone else, some charitable townsfolk would have hitched a wagon to their least excitable horse and rescued him from his misery, but because of who he was and the crimes he was suspected of having committed, no one made the effort.

Instead they all watched as the stranger struggled down the road toward them. The glow of his lantern continued to sway back and forth as he moved closer until a flash of lightning came from the sky just above him, and suddenly the light went out. To everyone, it appeared that a powerful bolt from the sky had struck the stranger down, but no one went out to see if he was still alive. This was, they felt, God's justice and it was not their place to question it.

By the next morning the storm had passed and it was safe to go outside. A group of men went out to discover what had happened to the stranger and they found his body in the middle of the road. They threw his remains in an unmarked grave and felt relieved that they would never see his like in Knob Noster again. In all likelihood, he would have been forgotten were it not for what followed soon thereafter.

Just a week after the hermit's death a visitor, whose appearance shocked all those who saw him, arrived in Knob Noster. It was Daniel, still alive and looking very fine in clothes one would never expect to see worn by a slave. Jaws dropped when he walked inside the town store with a silver-topped cane in his hand.

"Excuse me," he said to the shop's owner, a man whom he had dealt with often years ago. "Have you seen Mr. Cochran? I just visited his home and he wasn't there."

"Mr. Cochran?" asked the shopkeeper. "I've never heard of a Mr. Cochran around here."

Daniel seemed surprised by this. "I know for a fact that he comes to this very store on occasion to buy supplies."

"You don't mean the hermit?"

Daniel considered this for a moment. "I suppose he does keep to himself a lot, but I wouldn't have gone so far as to call him a hermit. He's a very kind man."

"Kind?" asked the shopkeeper, who was unable to imagine this particular word being used to describe the stranger.

"More so than that," Daniel replied. "He is the most generous man I've ever known. I would not be here today if it weren't for him. You see I was born in chains and taken from my family so I could be sold to a man of notorious cruelty named Kenneth Cochran."

"I thought you said he was kind?"

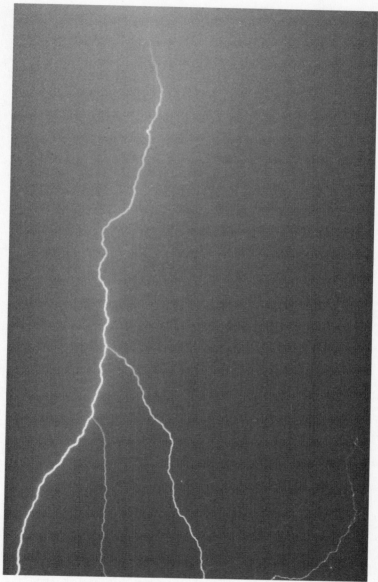

The storm that erupted was the most destructive and violent of any they had ever seen.

"Kenneth Cochran was Mr. Cochran's father. Though they looked very much alike, they were very different people. Mr. Cochran's father thought his son to be a weak-willed wretch and browbeat him every chance he got, which is why the man you call a hermit finds it so hard to talk to others. Despite his incredible shyness he was shrewd enough to make some fine investments, which earned him a small fortune that allowed him to become independent from his father. He used part of his fortune to buy my freedom. He then offered to educate me so that I could make a fortune of my own someday. Together we moved to the small cottage just outside of this town, and he first taught me how to read and cipher and then how to use these skills to make myself a better man."

"But we thought you were his slave?"

Daniel shook his head. "I was his student, who was only too happy to repay his kindness by performing chores for him around his house. I suspect that it is the color of my skin that caused you to suspect that I did this for any other reason."

"But if you were always free, why did you leave? We thought he had murdered you."

Daniel was shocked to hear this. "Mr. Cochran couldn't hurt a fly, much less take the life of another man. No, he told me that I had learned everything he could teach me, so it was now time for me to go out into the world on my own. I did so and, thanks to his teachings, have become very successful in business. I have come back to see him to thank him and to show him what his generosity has wrought."

The shopkeeper was almost too overcome by what he had just heard to speak. "We thought he was a murderer and a thief," he insisted. "We didn't know!"

"What happened? Tell me what happened," Daniel said sternly.

When the shopkeeper told him, Daniel was horrified by the news.

"Don't you see!" he shouted at the shopkeeper. "He was alone and afraid! He came to you so that he would not suffer in the storm by himself and you left him to die because you were too ignorant to even try and find out what he was really like! You judged him without knowing any of the facts and with this judgment you killed him as surely as you would have by hanging him with a noose!"

"We didn't know," the shopkeeper said weakly in his defense.

"Well, know this," said Daniel. "The crime you have committed is not one that will go unpunished. Just you wait. You have not seen the last of the hermit you left to die."

Daniel then turned away from the store's counter and walked out of it forever. It was the last time anyone ever saw him in the town again.

Word soon spread about the true identity of the stranger, and though many of those who misjudged him felt guilty over what they had done, most of the towns-people chose to blame the hermit instead. He shouldn't have been so secretive, they insisted. And it would have helped if he had taken the occasional bath.

As for Daniel's warning about Mr. Cochran, it was not an idle threat. Not long after the truth was revealed, another storm lit up the town's sky. Not as fierce as the last, it was still quite powerful and kept everyone inside. Just as before, they sat by their windows and watched as nature put on an incredible show; then, they spotted something in the distance that they knew had nothing to do with the natural world.

Far off along the road that led outside of town they saw the glow of a lamp, which swung from side to side as if it were being carried by hand. Not ready to make the same mistake twice, a group of men went out by wagon to meet up with this figure in the storm. They rode toward the light, but when they at last reached it, it vanished as if it had never been there. At once they knew what they had seen. It was the ghost of the stranger who had returned from the grave to remind them of what they had done.

From then on, to this very day, the ghost of the hermit of Knob Noster can be seen during every storm that hits the town, swinging his lamp along the road where he died trying to reach the people who had never even bothered to ask him his name.

The Ozark Madonna

The Vidors were avid hikers who regularly left their St. Louis home to travel around the state and explore all of its wilderness areas. In 1996 they took their first trip to the Mark Twain National Forest so they could walk along the Ozark Mountains. The forest turned out to be even more beautiful than they had imagined, so two years later they decided to go there again. It was during this second visit that they caught a glimpse of the area's most famous ghost.

They were walking along a trail when Jacob looked up and saw what he thought was a woman standing on a mountain ridge top.

"Look up there," he said to his wife Jessica, pointing up to the ridge.

"How'd she get up there?" Jessica asked when she caught sight of the woman. "She must be a really good climber."

As they moved closer they saw that she was holding something in her arms.

"Is that—" Jessica started to say. "No," she decided. "It couldn't be."

"It sure looks like it," said Jacob.

"But how could she climb up there with a baby in her arms?"

"I don't know. Maybe she had one of those sling things."

"Even so, there's no way she could make a climb like that with a baby."

From a distance they heard the sound of a baby's cries.

"I guess she found a way," said Jacob.

From a distance they heard the sound of a baby's cries.

"If she did, someone should alert the authorities. No sane person would risk their child's life by taking them up a mountain like that."

Jessica decided to get the woman's attention. "Hey, you!"

"What are you doing?" asked Jacob.

"I'm giving this lady a piece of my mind," answered Jessica.

"Aw, Jess. Leave her alone. She's obviously a local. They do things their own way. And for all we know there's a trail that leads to that spot that we can't see."

"Nonsense," said Jessica. "Hey! You!" she shouted again.

"I don't think she's paying any attention to you," said Jacob when the woman completely failed to react to his wife's calls.

Jessica ignored him and continued. "What do you think you're doing? You can't climb up a mountain with a baby!"

This time Jessica finally caught the woman's attention. The woman stopped and stared down at the Vidors.

"See," said Jessica, "she can hear me." Jessica was about to shout at her again when the woman did something so shocking that both she and Jacob were rendered completely speechless.

The woman vanished. She faded from sight right in front of their eyes, taking her baby with her.

The Vidors stood still and silent for several minutes before they could speak again.

"Did you—" he stammered.

"Yes," she answered before he could finish.

"She just—"

"She did."

"Like she wasn't—"

"Even there."

"We better—"

"Head back to camp. That's a good idea."

The two of them turned slowly around and hiked the five miles back to their campsite. Once they got there they pretended like everything was normal and started their supper, but neither of them could concentrate, so they decided to drive down to the nearest town and see if they could find some place to eat.

They ended up at a broken down diner. It was a place that hadn't changed a bit since it had been first built 50 years ago. The two of them sat quietly in one of the booths and poked disinterestedly at the food in front of them.

"What's the matter with you two?" asked the waitress wearing a nametag marked Rose.

They looked at each other. Neither one of them wanted anyone to think they were crazy, but the tension of keeping what they had seen to themselves was too much for them to bear. In a quick burst of words they told Rose what they had seen that afternoon.

"Oh, that's nothing to worry about," Rose said. "You just saw Laurie May."

"Laurie May?" asked Jacob.

"Sure. Laurie May Maumsey. She's been haunting the Ozarks for 60 years."

"Are you talking about Laurie May?" asked a grizzled looking older man who was sitting on a stool at the counter.

"These two saw her today," Rose said as she nodded at him.

"I saw her once. Did you see her feet?" he asked the Vidors.

"No," answered Jacob.

"They were completely bare when I spotted her. I couldn't believe that she could have walked to where she was in bare feet—they should have been scratched up or cut to ribbons, but they weren't. Then she just faded away right in front of me and it suddenly made sense."

"Where did she come from?" asked Jessica.

"Hereabouts, far as I've heard," answered the old man.

"No, I mean how did she become a ghost?"

"Same way as everyone else does. She died."

Jessica was starting to lose her patience. Normally she loved to talk to colorful locals, but this guy was getting on her nerves.

"How did she die?" she asked one more time. She was ready to smack him if he said something like "Stopped breathing, I suppose."

But he didn't say that. Instead he just sighed and shook his head. "It's a very sad story," he warned them. "The kind that can make you forget just how wonderful this world of ours can really be."

*　　*　　*

Laurie May Comshaw found out that she was marrying John Maumsey when she came home from what turned out to be her last day of school. She was 13. John and Laurie May's father were acquaintances who had met because John was a bootlegger and her father was an alcoholic. They had just come to an arrangement. John wouldn't beat her father to death for the money he owed him, if her father gave him Laurie May to settle the debt.

Life for Laurie May became really hard after that.

Despite the fact that bootlegging was a booming profession in the years before the end of Prohibition, John never had any money, and so their life was one of constant poverty. There were two major reasons for this: first, John liked to drink his goods more than he liked to sell them and second, he was very, very stupid. Even during those rare moments when he was sober enough to earn some cash, he invariably handed it over to someone who insisted that the money could be used to make him richer. No matter how many times he got ripped off, it never occurred to him that he had earned the reputation for being the biggest sucker in the state.

Had he ever found out about his reputation, he would have reacted to the news with a furious rage. That's how he reacted to everything. His fuse was so short, its very existence was in question. He lost his temper at least twice every hour and he frequently lashed out violently when he did. Poor Laurie May was the person who most often suffered from his constant volatility. There wasn't a moment in their entire marriage when she didn't sport an ugly bruise somewhere on her body.

A quiet girl, Laurie May did everything she could to accept her horrible fate. All that she asked for, when she prayed at night, was for a baby she could love. Love was something that had always been missing from her life, but she knew she wanted a child to love and nurture.

Unfortunately, John's violent ways kept her prayers from being answered. She miscarried three times after suffering vicious beatings at his hands and she despaired that she would never be able to carry a baby to term.

Then a small miracle happened; John got arrested for assault and was sentenced to a year in prison. And while he was gone, his son, Luke, was born.

Life was still incredibly hard for Laurie May. She had little left of the money they had, and with John gone there was no one to earn more. But she struggled through with a determination she didn't know she had in her. She couldn't even afford to buy shoes for her feet, but she kept Luke fed and healthy, and was happy at last about having something in her life worth being happy about.

When John was released, her happiness was extinguished in a single night.

He came back home drunk and looking for money for more booze. All Laurie May had was the money she needed to take care of her baby. Not the nurturing type, John told her to give it to him. She refused. He slapped her to the ground, but she refused to change her mind. He beat her some more, but it soon became evident that she wasn't going to tell him where she kept their meager savings.

"Give me that money!" he yelled at her angrily. "I'm your husband and when I tell you to do something you do it, dammit!"

She stayed quiet.

"Fine, then," he said. "If I can't whup it out of you, maybe I can whup it out of the kid." John moved toward his infant son, who was busy crying in an ancient bassinette.

"No!" she screamed. With speed she didn't know she possessed, she ran to the bassinette for her son before John could reach him.

"Give me that money or something bad is going to happen to that kid," John threatened her.

"You wouldn't. Even you wouldn't be *that* low."

"I said give me that money!" John shouted as he grabbed her by her arms.

Luke screamed in his mother's arms as his father shook the two of them around their tiny shack of a cabin. Then, at once, his screaming stopped. In the struggle the child had slipped from Laurie May's arms onto the cold stone floor below.

John left with the few dollars he had fought so hard to get, while Laurie May wept and cradled her all-too-silent child. The next day she buried him out back behind their cabin and on the following day she slipped her neck into a homemade noose before John got home.

*   *   *

"From what I reckon," the old man told the Vidors, "people started seeing her ghost about six months after she died. I caught my only glimpse of her 30 years back, but some folks have seen her more than once. They say she always looks the same. Terribly sad, holding that baby of hers like it was the only thing in the world that ever mattered. Do you know what they call her?"

"No, what?" asked Jessica.

"The Ozark Madonna. Some folks think it's blasphemous to call her that, but those of us who've seen her…well…we know it fits."

"What happened to John?" asked Jacob.

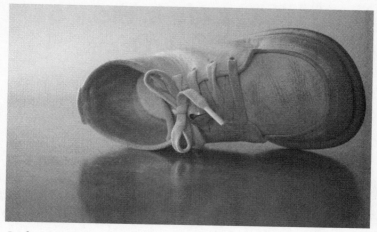

In the struggle the child had slipped from Laurie May's arms onto the cold stone floor.

"I don't know," the old man admitted. "But I suspect that whatever did happen to him it wasn't as bad as he deserved. With any luck though, he's now in a place where he suffers more than Laurie May ever did."

"Amen," said Rose.

When the Vidors returned to their campsite that night, they had a choice to make. Either they could continue their vacation like they had planned and keep hiking through the Ozarks, even if it meant possibly having another run-in with the Ozark Madonna, or they could just go home.

They chose to stay.

They never did see the ghost of Laurie May again, but even if they had, they wouldn't have been frightened. Instead they would have just smiled at her and waved her on.

The Lady in the Long Black Dress

Alphonse Templeton was a very large man. At 6'5" and 300 pounds he was the biggest man in Paris, Missouri, and he feared no man. But he was afraid on one particular night. It was a cold evening and ice was just starting to form on the streets. Alphonse was alone, a mile away from his house. He had stayed too long at the local tavern and had been too drunk to consider the consequences of staying out so late, but now that he was outside he was sober enough to fear what might meet him on his way.

He tried to walk as quickly as he could, but the ice made his journey treacherous and he slipped and fell several times along the way. Luckily the full moon was out that night, so he could at least see where he was going. After slipping for a third time, he decided to stop walking and instead slid along the ice, never taking his feet off of the ground. He managed to gain some momentum and starting speeding along the road toward his house.

But then his shoe hit a stone and he tumbled head first to the ground below. He felt a sudden jolt of pain followed by the warm wet feeling of blood trickling down his face.

"Blast it!" he swore as he gingerly held his hand up to his injured nose. He swore even louder when he touched it and another rocketing jolt of pain surged straight to his nervous system. He reached into his pocket, found an old handkerchief and used it to stanch the flow of the blood as he once again starting walking carefully on the icy road.

Distracted by the pain, he failed to notice the figure of a person walking toward him, but when he looked up and saw who it was, he immediately forgot about his nose and turned to run in the opposite direction. His feet hit a glassy sheet of ice and slipped out from under him. This time he fell straight on his back, the impact taking all of the wind from his lungs. He tried to get up, but the sudden ringing sensation in his head kept him on the ground.

He closed his eyes tight and held his breath as the figure came closer to his prone body, hoping that whatever happened, it would be over quickly. Seconds passed like minutes until he could not anticipate it any longer, and he breathed in deeply, opened his eyes and watched as a woman in a long black dress and a long veiled hat walked past him. In her hand she held a silver-topped cane, which—like her feet—never seemed to touch the ground.

Alphonse began to scream, but his cries failed to capture the spirit's attention. It didn't even look down at him as it passed. It simply carried on moving down the road, as if the sight of a large man lying on his back, bleeding in the middle of the road at night was too common an occurrence even to glance at.

The large man sighed with relief. He slowly struggled to his feet and made his way home, where he awakened his sleeping wife and told her how he had bravely confronted the town's famous Lady in Black.

*   *   *

It all began one cold autumn evening, just a few months after the end of the Civil War. A young mother named Darcy Ambrose was in her front yard calling for her children to come home when a woman she had never seen before walked past her along the street. The woman was dressed in a widow's garb: a long black dress and a large black hat with a veil that draped down on her face, along with a fancy silver-topped cane.

That first night Darcy thought nothing of the woman and assumed that she had probably come to Paris to reunite with a son or husband who was returning from the war. Given what she was wearing, Darcy thought perhaps she had come to collect a fallen soldier's remains to take home for a proper burial. But her opinion quickly changed when she saw the woman the next night. This time she studied the walking woman a bit more carefully and was shocked to notice that—in a manner she could not explain—the Lady in Black's feet never seemed to touch the ground. Horrified, she ran into her house and stayed there until morning. The next day she went out and told everyone she knew what she had seen the previous night. At first many thought she was suffering some sort of mental breakdown, but when others starting seeing the same woman around town, it quickly became clear that the town of Paris was being haunted by the spirit of a woman that no one could identify.

Though there was no evidence that the spirit's intentions were evil or that the spirit posed a threat to anyone it came across, the town as a whole reacted with a collective rush of terror. People refused to travel in town alone, children were kept inside, and doors and windows were kept firmly locked at all times. Sightings of the Lady in Black continued, and though she could often be seen

The Lady in Black's feet never seemed to touch the ground.

waving her silver-topped cane, she never once did anything that justified the town's extreme reaction to her presence.

Fall soon turned to winter and then winter turned to spring. Once the weather turned warm, all sightings of the spirit ceased. Everyone in Paris breathed a collective sigh of relief, assuming that the Lady in Black was gone for good. But when October came around the spirit returned and walked the town's streets until the end of March. This continued for decades, all the way until 1934, when—just as mysteriously as she had arrived—the spirit vanished that March and never again returned.

*   *   *

Louisa Beatty and Andrew Davidson had been engaged for three months when he enlisted to fight in the Union army. The two of them had met in her birthplace of Albany, New York, but they planned—when Andrew returned from the war—to return to his hometown, Paris, Missouri. Always a frail woman, Louisa took ill not long after Andrew left Albany to join his regiment. Her doctor could not determine what was wrong with her, so he ordered her—to be on the safe side—to take an extended bed rest.

She stayed in bed for six months and only grew weaker and weaker as the days went on. The muscles in her left leg withered to the point that—on those rare occasions she did leave her bed—she needed a cane to walk. As the months passed, her doctor still could not diagnose the cause of her illness. Members of her family started to speculate that her sickness may have been more mental than physical—brought on by the separation from her fiancé and her constant fears for his well-being. Everyday she would ask if anyone had heard any news from him, if any letters from him had arrived, and each day they would tell her that they had heard nothing and that no letters had come. This, they believed, was the true cause of her infirmity.

Finally, nearly a year after he had left, a letter finally arrived from Andrew for Louisa, and its contents proved to be as harmful as a vial full of arsenic. It read:

Dear Louisa,

I apologize for the lateness of this letter and that I did not write to you sooner, but circumstances made it impossible for me to contact you. Two months after I left Albany, my regiment was slaughtered in a surprise Confederate attack. I was wounded and left for dead, but I was found and nursed back to health by a local family here in Virginia. During that time I got to know their eldest daughter, Sophie, and lost my heart to her. We are to be married in three months. I hope you can forgive me for ending our engagement in this manner, but I understand if you cannot. You are a beautiful girl and I suspect that this news only serves to free your hand to any of your many former suitors, so it is likely you will find my replacement without any difficulty. Whoever this lucky gentleman is, I wish the both of you the best of luck and a life filled with happiness.

With regrets,
Andrew

Louisa never recovered from this unexpected blow. Within a month of receiving the letter she was only hours away from her death. Knowing she had very little time left, she told her sister, Eileen, that she had cursed both Andrew and the town he had come from.

"I shall haunt them both," she said in a weak whisper. "I will wear the clothes of a widow, to remind him of the promise he so callously broke. I will haunt him in the spring and the summer and I shall haunt that place which spawned him in the autumn and winter, and I will not stop until he is dead."

Andrew Davidson died at the age of 94 in 1934, the same year the Lady in Black failed to return to Paris. At least that's how this version of the legend goes.

*   *   *

According to some, there is another more earthbound answer as to why the Lady in Black disappeared forever that year. Many believed that she was never a ghost in the first place, but instead an eccentric woman whose strange attire confused the town into thinking she was a spirit from beyond.

The leading proponent of this theory was the former editor of the *Monroe County Appeal*, Si Colburn. He believed that the Lady in Black was a spinster he had met when he first moved to Paris in 1920. Like Louisa in the legend, this old woman had suffered the indignity of having her fiancé run out on her before their marriage (although Si was quick to point out that, given the woman's general demeanor, running out on her was something any sensible man would have done). She took to wearing black from that point on, and, being over six feet tall, she was a formidable looking figure wherever she went. Her death in 1934 explained why that was the last year anyone saw the Lady in Black.

Though entirely logical, this explanation fails to take several important factors into account. First, there were the numerous reports from people who saw the ghost saying that its feet never touched the ground. Second, it is hard to believe that this woman—as eccentric as she was—could spend 70 years of her life in Paris and be confused for a ghost all that time. And why was she only seen in town at night during the fall and winter? Did she travel every year to another place during the spring and summer months? Was there a reason she only went outside after dark?

The streets of Paris are now free of any ghosts, but the mystery of just who the Lady in Black really was remains unsolved to this day. Was the Lady in Black the ghost of a spurned woman, or just a flesh and blood spurned woman whose eccentric manner and dress confused and bewildered her fellow townspeople for nearly 70 years?

No one knows for sure, but it is certainly fun to think about.

4
Rambunctious Spirits

Roberta Steel

It was a perfect day outside. The sun was shining, the birds were singing and the sky was a vast blue sea without a single cloud in sight. It was the kind of day that the students at Northwest Missouri State had been dreaming about after nearly a month of drab rainy days, but—almost as if to spite them—it had come just before midterms, which meant most of them could only watch it from their windows as they sat and studied in their dorm rooms.

Roberta Steel felt the warm rays of the sunshine on her arm as she tried to read an exceedingly boring chapter in her incredibly boring textbook about the Civil War. Somehow the author of the textbook had taken one of the most fascinating periods of American history and turned it into the literary equivalent of warm milk. Roberta struggled not to fall asleep as her eyes glazed over a bone-dry paragraph describing the events leading up to the Battle of Gettysburg.

With a quick shake of her head, she brought herself out of her drowsy gaze and looked longingly out of her window. Only a small handful of students stood out in the middle of the school's lush green campus. They were either extremely confident in their ability to pass their midterms or they were too entranced by this gift of sunshine to care. Roberta desperately wanted to join them, but she was close to failing her history class, so she needed a good mark on this exam to salvage her grade. The closest she could come to the outdoors was to open her window. A cool breeze blew into her room and instantly made her feel better. She then picked the book back up and once more tried to make her way through it.

To those that knew her, Roberta was a kind, generous soul who seemed slightly out of place at the university. She had the cheerful demeanor of the kind of girl who usually got married right out of high school and took to being an instant housewife. It was 1951, after all, and it was the path followed by the majority of Roberta's friends, but she wanted to do something different. She wanted to be more than just a happy homemaker devoted to the needs of a husband and children; she wanted to be an individual who made a mark on the world all by herself, not as some man's wife.

The truth was that she had no idea how she was going to make this mark on the world or what she would do once she finished school, but she refused to let these trivial details get in the way of her ambitions. She had a dream and that was enough to keep her going. And to keep this dream alive she had to pass history.

She refused to be further distracted by the world that was buzzing with life and activity just outside her window. More students gave in to the sunshine and the campus slowly became filled with activity. The sounds of their revelry grew so distracting that finally Roberta had enough and turned to close the window, but she didn't make it in time.

It happened in less than an instant. There was no warning. The sound was heard only after it had occurred. The people on the campus who saw it cried out in horror, unable to believe their eyes.

She felt the warm rays of the sunshine on her arms as she tried to read her incredibly boring textbook.

There was no time for Roberta to react or scream. The flame shot through her open window and covered her entire body. The pain was so intense her system could not handle it. She fell to the floor as pieces of her hair and skin floated in the air around her. In less than a single second—in the time that passes in the blink of an eye—all of Roberta's ambitions ended, all of her dreams turned to tinder. The fire changed everything, and she didn't even know it had happened.

*   *   *

Just below her window a propane tank had exploded. The force of the blast had rocketed the tank 100 feet into the air. Besides Roberta, four other students had been injured by this sudden explosion, but she had received the worst of it. Over 75% of her body was covered in second-degree burns. The reason why she suffered the most? She had been the only student with her window open.

It is the kind of pain that most of us are lucky enough not to experience; it is hard to even imagine such pain. Think of the pain that resulted the last time your hand accidentally brushed against a red-hot stove element for just a second. Now multiply that by a thousand and you still do not even come close to describing the agony of a person unfortunate to be as badly burned as Roberta was.

Most people in her condition die very quickly. Given the choice between agony and death, few have the strength to choose the former knowing the promise of peace that comes with the latter. But Roberta was not like most people. She lingered in Maryville's St. Joseph's Hospital for 11 days before she finally stopped fighting her hopeless battle to survive. And for most people this would be the end of her story, but, once again, Roberta was not like most people.

*   *   *

For one thing, most people don't get buildings named after them, but Roberta did. The university renamed the dormitory in which she lived, Roberta Hall. We can wonder whether Roberta would have been honored to be remembered this way or if she would be insulted to have the place where all her dreams ended be given her name. Either way, Roberta chose not to leave the building and has remained there ever since.

The dorm's residents first noticed her presence in the months that followed her passing. It all started when doors and windows began to lock and unlock themselves at all hours of the day. Lights would turn on suddenly and then switch off just as quickly. Thumping noises could be heard from within the walls.

For a time all of these incidents were shrugged off as someone's idea of a practical joke, but then people started hearing the music and it became clear that there was more to all of this than some silly prank.

From deep inside the basement, the sound of sad, mournful piano melodies were heard coming from a room that had been empty for years and had never once contained a piano. Throughout her short life Roberta had been an avid amateur musician, but she had always preferred faster, more upbeat tunes. It was clear from these phantom melodies that Roberta was not happy with her twist of fate and was extremely melancholy.

In time the residents of Roberta Hall were doing more than unlocking mysteriously locked doors and listening to sad songs from the afterlife; they were seeing things too.

One resident named Monica was standing outside the building when she saw a brown-haired woman standing at a window on a higher floor. The woman looked familiar, like the person in the portrait that hung in the lobby, but Monica was less concerned about this resemblance than by the fact that the woman was standing where she was in the first place. Monica had been in that particular room and knew that it would have been impossible for a person to stand by the window, given the way the furniture in the room was organized.

Another resident named Amy woke up one night and saw what looked like the silhouette of a young woman in the bathroom she shared with her roommate. She assumed that her roommate was up in the middle of the night when she heard the toilet flush, but then noticed her still sleeping in her bed on the other side of the room. Confused, Amy got up to investigate and found that the bathroom was now completely empty.

Not long after this, the women who lived in Roberta Hall started a tradition of using curling irons to leave burn marks on their bedroom doors. The idea behind this unique tradition was that Roberta, seeing the scorched wood, would be frightened away. No one wanted anything to do with Roberta once word of what happened to two girls named Leslie and Jean got around.

There are several kinds of roommate relationships you can have when fate pairs you up at random to share a space with another person. You can become friends, enemies or indifferent acquaintances, depending on how well fate made the match. Jean and Leslie were the last of these three types, having decided early on to have as little contact with each other as was humanly possible. They hardly ever spoke to each other and didn't even know what the other's major was.

On one particular evening it was a shock to Leslie when, during a loud thunderstorm, she felt someone slip into her bed and wrap her arms around her. She quickly turned to face her roommate and question this highly inappropriate act, but before she could get a word out, she discovered that she was alone in her bed and Jean was still sleeping across the room.

Terrified, she jumped out of her bed and ripped off its sheets, revealing it to be completely bare. "What the—" she swore aloud, unable to comprehend what had just happened to her.

"What are you doing?" Jean mumbled behind her.

"Nothing," she answered weakly. "I just…had a bad dream, I guess."

"Well, keep it down, will you," Jean muttered into her pillow. "Some of us have exams in the morning."

Leslie hesitantly remade her bed and got back under the covers. The rain and thunder outside only made it that much harder for her to calm down.

An hour passed and Jean was dreaming about her upcoming philosophy exam. She had heard a rumor that the professor had once given an exam that consisted of a one-word question, "Why?" and the only person who received an A had done so by simply answering, "Why not?" In her dream, Jean was about to receive her quiz booklet and she was hoping for the one-word exam when she felt someone slip into her bed and embrace her.

Jean responded by kicking at the person as hard as she could, rocketing the intruder off of the bed. She heard a loud thump on the floor, which was followed by the voice of her roommate.

"What the hell was that?" asked Leslie.

Jean, now awake, looked to see who she had just booted to the floor. She turned on her bedside lamp, and looked down and saw the woman whose portrait graced Roberta Hall's lobby—it was Roberta Steel herself and she hadn't taken kindly to Jean's violent rejection. The angry phantom leapt to its vaguely defined feet and started running like a crazy person around the room. Though the spirit made no sound, it was clear that it was trying to scream. It ran faster and faster around the room, until it moved so fast that it started to pull itself apart and finally vanished in a wisp of smoke.

Since then, her appearances in the hall have been much less extreme. Perhaps the curling iron trick was working, but doors and windows still locked themselves shut without notice. Music can still be heard coming from the basement along with those thumping noises through the walls of Roberta Hall.

Roberta Steel always wanted to be special. In life she didn't get to see this happen, but at least in death she was able to earn some of that renown she had dreamed of someday achieving. Perhaps it's more infamy than she may have wanted, but it's more than a lot of people get and, truthfully, probably more than she would have gotten if she had only closed her window just a minute earlier.

St. Louis Hotels

Every time you step into a hotel room you are entering a place of mystery. Depending on how old the hotel is, it could be a room that has held hundreds, even thousands, of different people over the years, and though it may shock some of you to hear it, not all of those people left those rooms alive.

Death is a fact of life in the hospitality business, albeit one that is never mentioned in any hotel's brochure. Thanks to sudden strokes, heart attacks, suicides, overdoses and even murder, people's lives ended in hotel rooms all the time. Remember that room you stayed in during your last vacation? There is a chance that someone may have died in that very bed you slept on (although— unless it was a *very bad* hotel—it's unlikely that you shared the same sheets), or if not the bed, then maybe the bathtub or the chair by the door. There is no way for you to know for sure. You could always ask the concierge, but it's not in their best interest to tell you the truth and— depending on how long they've worked there—they may not even know the truth in the first place.

Now before you decide to never go on vacation ever again, remember that just because someone could have died in a hotel room doesn't mean that someone actually did, and since you have no way to know for certain, there's no point in getting worked up about it. Well, that's not completely true. There is *one* way to know for certain, but it's one that would leave most people looking back fondly at their previous ignorance.

Back in 1980 a salesman named Larry Brooks walked into room 304 of the Chase Hotel in St. Louis. Tired after a long trip, he just had a few more hours before he had to get up for a meeting with a client in the morning, so he was less than thrilled to discover a woman standing in the room, looking out the window. In Larry's line of work it wasn't uncommon for clients looking for good deals to sweeten him up by sending attractive call girls to entertain him, but Larry was a faithful family man. He would never cheat on his wife, and even if he wanted to, he was often too exhausted during these trips to do anything with these girls.

But, as much as he hated to admit it, he was tempted that night. The girl was a gorgeous redhead dressed in an old-fashioned gown made out of white chiffon. She looked like a movie star from the 1940s and it took him a moment to speak after he watched her pass by.

"Uh, hi," he mumbled shyly. His cheeks turned red with discomfort.

She turned away from the window and just looked at him with an enigmatic smile.

"The thing is," he continued, "I don't know what Craig told you, but I'm a married man and I have to get up in four and a half hours, so I'm not going to need your…uh…services…tonight."

If she heard him, she didn't show it. Instead she continued to look out the window with the same small, indecipherable smile etched on her face.

"So," he continued to say, "I would really appreciate it if you left. Feel free to keep whatever Craig paid you. No questions asked."

He waited for some sign that she was listening to what he was saying, but there was nothing except an uncomfortable silence.

"Look," he said sharply, "I have no time for this nonsense, so will you please just leave."

She didn't move.

He rolled his eyes. "Fine. Do you want more money? I've got 50 bucks in my wallet. It's yours if you go right now."

Nothing.

"Fine," he said. "I'm going to call downstairs and have someone escort you out of here."

She still showed no sign of distress.

Exasperated, he turned away from the beautiful intruder and picked up the phone and called the front desk.

"Hi," he sighed, "this is Larry Brooks in room 304 and—"

"There's a woman in your room," said the night clerk.

"That's right," said Larry. "How did you know?"

"Don't worry about her," the clerk continued to say, ignoring Larry's question. "She's gone now."

"What are you talking about?" asked Larry. "She's right here."

He turned around to look at her.

On the other end of the line, the clerk heard the sound—by now familiar to him—of the phone's receiver hitting the room's thick carpet.

"Told you," he said just before he hung up.

Back in his room, Larry couldn't believe his own eyes. The beautiful young redhead who had been standing at

She looked like a movie star from the 1940s.

his window just a few seconds before was gone. The window was still closed and there was no way she could have reached the door without him seeing her go.

He was so confused, and now annoyed, that he bent over and picked up the phone's receiver from the floor and called the front desk again.

"Why didn't you tell me the room was haunted?" he asked angrily the very second the night clerk answered his phone. Somehow he could imagine the clerk shrugging, three stories below.

"You didn't ask," the clerk answered matter-of-factly. "Do you want another room?"

"No," Larry answered. "But next time just warn a guy that he might open his door to a gorgeous redheaded ghost. I thought she was a hooker for cripes' sake."

"Will do," answered the clerk. "Is there anything else I can help you with?"

"No," said Larry. "Sorry I shouted at you."

"No problem. Have a good night."

"You too." Larry hung up his phone and climbed onto his bed. He was so tired he couldn't even be bothered to take off his clothes. It was only as he started to fall asleep that it occurred to him that the girl he had just seen probably died in this room and may have even died on the bed he was lying on, but at that point he was too tired to care.

He never did find out who the girl was or how she came to haunt that room in that hotel, but he always made sure for the rest of his travels to ask each clerk who checked him in if he could expect to find a ghost in his room.

*   *   *

Then again, just because you see a ghost in your hotel room doesn't mean that the person whom the spirit belonged to actually died there. It doesn't even mean that the spirit had ever even been in that room, much less that particular hotel. This fact is illustrated by another strange incident that occurred in another St. Louis hotel, 113 years before Larry Brooks had his encounter with the redheaded stranger.

It happened at the Pacific House Hotel in 1867, and also involved a salesman. His name was George Price and he was from Boston. Unlike Larry, he had actually spent some time in his room before he had his paranormal experience, having been there for three weeks by the time it happened. By then he had grown tired of St. Louis and yearned to return to his family, but his job required him to stay in town for another week. And most likely it was this desire of his to be reunited with his kin that led to what happened that strange night. It is the only explanation that seems to make any sense.

He had just returned from the same nearby restaurant where he had eaten every day since he arrived in town and was ready to go to bed. With a long yawn, he started changing out of his suit and into his pajamas when he felt a sudden feeling of warmth overtake him and the room. He could feel the source of this heat on his back, so he turned around to face it. What he saw made him wonder if he had already fallen asleep and was dreaming.

It was his little sister, Christina, which meant it absolutely had to be a dream. She was dead and had been for eight months now. She died at the age of 18 with a case of cholera. But despite these cold hard facts, she stood before him in his room with a gentle smile on her face.

George stood stunned and realized that what he was seeing was not his sister but her spirit. He could tell because her feet did not touch the floor, and because she was surrounded by a gray, misty haze that was not like anything he had ever encountered in the natural world.

He started to talk to her, but she shook her head to silence him. She could not speak, so she couldn't answer any of his questions. Instead she just smiled in a way that told him she was okay and that he shouldn't worry about her.

He burst into tears and as he cried he saw something he had never seen before on her cheek. It was a long scar that ran from just under her left eye to the corner of her mouth.

"What happened?" he asked her, pointing to her cheek. "Who did that to you?"

She just shook her head, with an expression indicating that it wasn't important and that she wasn't concerned about it.

"Are you sure you're okay?" he asked, even though he had no idea what he could have done if the answer was "No."

She just smiled and nodded and blew him a kiss as she began to slowly fade out of sight.

"No!" he protested. "Come back!"

But it was too late. She was gone.

The next morning George felt so dazed by the experience that a part of him really did believe he had simply dreamed the whole thing like he had first suspected. It wasn't until he returned home to Boston that he was finally convinced that what he saw that night had actually happened.

Visiting his parents, he told them about his experience with Christina in the hotel room, and when he told them about the scar on Christina's cheek, his mother gasped and dropped the cup of tea she had been holding.

"Mother, what's the matter?" he asked her, as she appeared visibly shaken in front of him.

"It was an accident," she insisted, tears welling up in her eyes.

"What was?" asked George's father.

"That undertaker was such a crook, I couldn't bear the thought of his touching my Christina," she told them. "I insisted on doing her burial makeup myself, but I forgot to take off my rings when I started and I accidentally scratched her face while I was applying the rouge."

"I didn't see any scratch," said her husband.

"I covered it up with more makeup. No one saw it. I'm the only person who knew it was there."

And so with this single revealed secret George learned that what had happened in the hotel had not been a dream but an actual encounter with the ghost of his sister. The revelation caused him to faint at his mother's feet. When he awoke, he took some relief in the fact that he was able to report to his parents that Christina appeared as radiant in her spirit form as she had been in life.

*   *   *

Now, chances are neither of these experiences is ever going to happen to you, no matter how many hotel rooms you stay in, but if something does happen, take heart in knowing that the anecdote you'll have is 1000 times better than even the nicest stolen hotel towel.

The White Lady

Were it not for a decision made by the men in charge of the Santa Fe Railroad in 1887, it is likely that the town of Marceline, Missouri, would not exist today. Before the railroad came and made the town home to a division point that routed trains headed to Chicago, it was a quiet farming community that had never had a lick of trouble. When the trains came and people arrived with them, the town wasn't ready—it didn't even have a sheriff, much less a jail. The newcomers were quick to take advantage of this and the town became a haven for violent men.

Marceline soon earned a reputation as a place where murder was an everyday occurrence and justice was not. Many who came to town took advantage of its lawlessness, committing crimes there that they knew they couldn't get away with anywhere else. Brent Briscoe was one of these men. He worked for the Santa Fe Railroad as a conductor and could have chosen any town along his line's route to live, but he chose Marceline because he had tired of the life of a family man.

He had met Juliet when she was a ticket clerk in Chicago. He had always liked her, but she was engaged to his friend Kent, so he kept his distance. But when her life took a bad turn, he was able to come to her rescue.

Juliet was pregnant, but Kent didn't want to be a father, so he disappeared. She was fired from her job for carrying an illegitimate child and evicted from her home, so Brent took her in and cared for her son like he was his own. For the first couple of months life was good, but it soon became very clear to Brent that Juliet had no feelings for him, and though she was grateful for his kindness, she would never love him. This made him bitter and his heart turned cold. He considered throwing her and her child back onto the street, but his thoughts became more sinister. He thought about murder, but he knew he would never get away with it as long as he lived in Chicago.

Then he heard about Marceline, Missouri.

In 1888 the three of them moved to the lawless town. Juliet and her baby lived there for only a week before they disappeared. Brent told everyone that she hated the small town and, with his help, she had moved back to Chicago where she had found an apartment and a new job.

The truth was that he had poisoned them and dropped their bodies into a nearby well. A month later he quit his job, moved away from Marceline and was never heard from again. His crime may have never been discovered, but a few months later the well was dug up during construction in the area and the bodies were found by a group of very surprised workmen. At first no one could identify the two bodies, but when an acquaintance of Brent's from the railroad heard about the case, they were able to put the pieces together.

No one made any attempt to find Brent, so Juliet and her son never received the justice that they deserved. Their bodies were buried in unmarked graves and a restaurant was built on the spot where their corpses had been found. It was called The Hole in the Wall Cafe and it was barely open for a week before the spirits of Juliet and her baby made themselves known.

The cafe's first cook heard the sound of a woman pleading for help and a baby crying from under the basement stairs. When he went to see who was there, he found nothing but an empty space. He found the incident so unsettling that he didn't even bother to give his notice, choosing instead to walk out of the cafe right then and there. He never came back.

As the months went on, many more of the restaurant's employees felt compelled to quit their jobs because of the unnerving sounds that could be heard in the basement. Things only got worse when the sounds were joined by a presence that was much more physical than anything else encountered in the basement before.

The White Lady was first spotted by a waitress named Lena. She had gone down to the basement to take a break and smoke a cigarette when she received the shock of her life. Taking a long first drag from the cigarette, she slowly exhaled, but she noticed that the smoke hovered in the air and then floated away as if it was being pulled by an invisible force. Her eyes followed the smoke as it grew in size and slowly took the shape of a woman in a white dress. She stood and gaped at the smoky phantom in front of her as it raised one of its wispy arms and pointed a finger in her direction. This was too much for Lena to take and she, just like the cafe's first cook, quit right then and there.

Still, as frightening as the encounter was, Lena got off very easily.

She lived.

Others would not be so lucky.

*   *   *

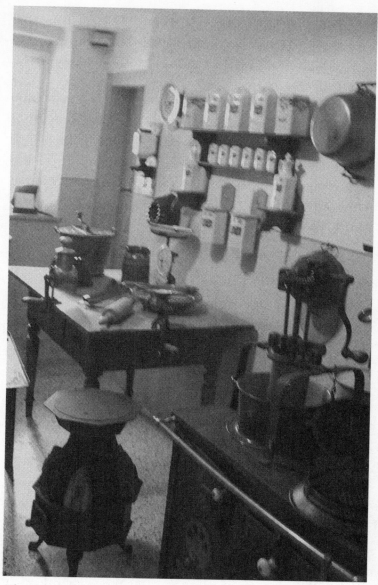

The Hole in the Wall Cafe was barely open for a week before the strange occurrences began.

All of the White Lady's victims had the same things in common. They all worked for the railroad; they all worked with Brent Briscoe; and they all died within hours of seeing her vengeful spirit.

Her first victim was Timothy Wise, an engineer who had been called into work to replace a fellow who had become suddenly ill. He was a friend of Eva, the cafe's owner, and she had allowed him to come in for breakfast before she usually opened. He was sitting at the counter while she cooked him some eggs, when the door to the basement burst open and they both saw the White Lady hovering above the ground in front of them. Just like before with Lena, the smoky phantom pointed her wispy finger at Timothy.

Just then the waitress arrived at the restaurant and immediately fainted when she saw the ghost confront the old engineer with a very unfriendly look. By the time Eva had revived her, the smoky wraith had faded away.

Timothy, unnerved by the experience, tried to get out of work that day, but he was told that there was no one else available to make the trip to Kansas City. Knowing his job was on the line, he went against his better judgment and got on the train. An hour later the train went off the tracks just outside the town of Rothville. He did not survive.

Her next victim was Wise's brother, Edrick, who died a year later when his train derailed at Bosworth, just two hours after he was confronted by the White Lady during a lunch at the cafe. Then came the death of a brakeman, who fell off the top of a boxcar after the vengeful spirit visited him while he was eating a plateful of pancakes.

Another victim was soon squashed between two boxcars the day he saw the White Lady pointing at him.

In each case, the White Lady seemed happy to serve as a harbinger of doom for men who worked in what was then a dangerous profession, but on at least two occasions it appeared that the wrathful spirit took matters into her own wispy hands.

The first case occurred in 1910, when an engineer named Breslin refused to be deterred by a visit from the now famous spirit. Though he knew what could happen to him if he returned to the railroad after seeing the White Lady, he decided to go back to work anyway, but he didn't quite make it. A half-hour after he left the cafe, he returned covered in his own blood. He collapsed on the floor, having been shot four times while he was on his way to the train station.

When he was asked who had shot him, he insisted that it had been the White Lady herself. The spirit had appeared in front of him with a gun and shot at him with six bullets, four of which met their mark. His story never changed once during the 24 hours he managed to live before he finally succumbed to his wounds.

A few years later another engineer named William Beach thought he had dodged a bullet when he made it home to Fort Madison, Iowa, safe and sound after he was visited by the White Lady. He had considered himself lucky, but several days later he was found shot dead in his bathtub. Based on the broken window in his bathroom, it was believed that the bullet had come from outside the house.

The last man to suffer the wrath of the White Lady was a brakeman named Fletcher. Of all of her victims, he was the only one to have never met Brent Briscoe, but he caught her attention when he attempted to prove to his friends and coworkers that she did not really exist.

"I ain't scared of any smoky spook," he declared to everyone during one breakfast at the cafe in 1917.

"Prove it," shouted one of his coworkers.

"Okay, I will," he answered. He then stood up and walked into the basement. "Here ghosty-ghosty-ghosty," he sang as he walked down the stairs.

He stayed down there for five minutes, but he wasn't singing anymore when he finally returned.

"Did you see anything?" asked one of his friends.

"No. I don't want to talk about it," he said, but the lack of color in his face suggested the contrary. Though his breakfast was still waiting in the booth where he had been sitting, he walked out of the restaurant, obviously in a hurry to get out as soon as he could.

Against his better instincts, he went to work that day and, just outside of Fort Madison, he tripped and fell underneath the train's wheels. Both of his legs were completely severed from his body and he died in the hospital several hours later.

The cafe burned down not too long after that, and the White Lady was never seen again. Many believed that she was gone for good because there was no one left in town who had had any connection with Brent Briscoe, so she no longer had the need for revenge. Others have suggested that she may have moved on, traveling along the rails in search of the one man she had truly wanted to point her wispy finger at all along.

Hopefully she found him.

The Gehm House

It hadn't been too long into the Furrys' marriage that the couple had decided it would be wise to sleep in separate bedrooms. Sam and Fanny loved each other and they didn't wish to be apart, but for the sake of their marriage they had to be. On several occasions immediately following their honeymoon, Sam was suddenly awakened by a powerful punch in the nose, but only on those nights when his wife was so exhausted that even the jet-plane roar of his nocturnal rumblings couldn't keep her awake. With the torturous combination of his earth-shaking snores and her frequent night terrors, whose sudden appearance in her unconscious caused her to engage in frantic and extremely violent battles in the middle of their bed, sleeping in separate rooms was a wise decision. In this way they managed to stay sane, a fact that they took into account when they went in search of a new home.

The year was 1956 and they had just found what they were looking for in the quiet St. Louis suburb of Webster Grove. It was a two-story house constructed of wood with a brick façade that was completely nondescript in a neighborhood where the architecture was kept as simple and tasteful as possible. The house had been built in 1890 by a fellow named Burt Adams, but the Furrys were not apprised of that fact. Nor were they told that its second owner was an eccentric fellow named Henry Gehm, who lived in the house until his death a dozen years earlier in 1944.

When they were first shown the house, all they were told was how much potential it had (it was a bit of a fixer-upper) and what a good neighborhood it was in. But what had clinched their decision to buy it was the fact that it had four bedrooms, one of which was far enough away from the others so that Sam's snores would only barely be heard by the rest of the family at night.

Fanny was relieved when they signed the deed of possession. "At last, I'm going to get some peace in bed."

But she didn't.

They had been in the house for a few months when she was awakened one night by the sensation of being shaken by a man's hands.

"Sweetie, stop it, I'm not in the mood," she mumbled sleepily without opening her eyes, assuming Sam had come in to engage in some late-night intimacy. But the shaking continued, so she opened her eyes and was shocked to discover that she was alone in the room. She quickly sat up and turned on her bedside lamp. It was 2:00 AM according to her alarm clock.

Must have been one of my nightmares, she told herself, even though she couldn't recall dreaming any of the various scenarios that had been known to cause her to physically act out while sleeping. Still, it seemed like a reasonable explanation, so she turned off her light, went back to sleep and didn't think anything of the incident until the next night, when it happened again.

This time she bolted up, wide awake, saw that she was alone and that it was once again 2:00 AM. She decided it was odd, but she didn't feel the need to tell anyone about it. What happened the next night changed her mind.

SLAM! SLAM! SLAM!

It sounded like someone was destroying her bed's headboard with a sledgehammer. Terrified she waited for the sound to stop before she sat up and turned on her light. The noise had been so loud that she expected to see the headboard smashed to splinters, but she was stunned to discover that it was completely untouched. Sensing a strange pattern, she glanced back at her alarm clock. It was, as she had suspected, 2:00 AM.

She did not wait for morning to tell her husband what she had heard, choosing instead to throw on her robe and run downstairs to his room, where his snores were making almost as much noise as whatever strange presence was responsible for these 2:00 AM wake-up calls.

She shook him awake. "Honey, get up."

"What are you doing?" he protested sleepily. "It's the middle of the night."

"I know. It's two in the morning," she informed him. "I have something important to tell you."

He yawned as he sat up in his bed. "What?"

"The house is haunted."

"Have you been drinking?" he asked after he pondered this news for a short moment.

"No!" Fanny hit him in the arm, offended that he would even suggest that.

"Ow!" he said as he rubbed the spot where she hit him. "I'm just saying there was that one time—"

"That was six years ago and it was New Year's Eve."

"You thought we were being invaded by aliens."

Sensing a strange pattern, she glanced back at her alarm clock.

"Like I said, that was New Year's Eve and I had had a bit too much champagne. Anyone could have made that mistake," she said defensively.

"Anyone could have thought that the Johnsons were aliens?"

"In those circumstances, yes," she insisted. "You saw what Marjorie Johnson was wearing. Would a normal human being wear something that hideous? Anyway, that's not what I was talking about. The house is haunted."

"I'm sure you think so, sweetie," he said to her in that condescending tone people usually reserve for occasions when they are talking to crazy people. "But I'll bet you anything that if you go back to bed and sober up a little—"

"I'm not drunk!" she shouted as she hit him again in the arm.

"Stop hitting me!"

"I will when you stop talking to me like I'm a mental case."

"Keep your voice down," Sam interrupted. "Or you'll wake the kids."

This managed to calm her down a bit.

"I'm telling you strange things have happened in my room for three nights in a row. I honestly think there's a ghost in this house and if you make another drunk crack, I'll pop you one right on your nose."

"Okay, okay, so say you're right and the house is haunted. What do you want me to do about it at two in the morning?"

"I don't know, I just thought you would want to know."

"Do you think it's safe for you to return to your room?"

"I guess so," she answered and shrugged.

"Then why don't you go back to bed and we'll talk about this in a calm and rational manner tomorrow morning."

*   *   *

The next morning the subject of ghosts didn't come up. By the time Fanny woke up, showered and got dressed, she was too busy making breakfast and getting the kids off to school to think about what had happened to her. By the time she had a chance to remember, Sam was already on his way to work and she was alone in the house.

KERRRRR-RAAASSSSSSSSSHHHHHHHHHHHHH-HHH!!!!!!!!

The sound came so suddenly that it almost made her jump out of her own skin. She ran to see that the large sconce on their living room wall had fallen to the floor. She wondered if it was just the result of poor installation or something more supernatural in nature as she cleaned up the mess as best she could.

Not surprisingly, Sam decided it was the former, blaming the incident on the previous owner's incompetence as a handyman.

"Look at how shoddily he screwed that thing into the wall. It's a miracle it stayed up there as long as it did."

Fanny was unconvinced.

After a few weeks passed without incident, however, Fanny started to believe that maybe Sam had been right to be so skeptical, but then one night she was awakened by the same slamming noise she had heard before, and this time it was joined by the sound of something beating against her bedroom window. She turned and looked at her alarm clock and—like always—it was 2:00 AM.

Without any way to explain what was happening, she decided to just accept it and started wearing earplugs to bed at night. Years passed and they had another child—a daughter. The pressures of caring for a newborn made it impossible to notice anything that was even obviously supernatural happening in the house, so it wasn't until their youngest was three that Fanny once again became aware that there was a mysterious force lurking inside their home. And this time it was impossible to ignore.

It was a Sunday morning and she was making pancakes for breakfast. She was standing in front of the griddle, spatula in hand, when she felt someone tug on her housecoat. It was their youngest, Debbie.

"Mommy...who's that lady?" Debbie asked hesitantly.

Fanny turned back to the griddle to flip the pancakes before they burned. "What lady, sweetie?" she asked her daughter.

"The one in my room at night. And who's the little boy?"

Something about her daughter's question triggered a switch in Fanny's mind. At once she knew that it had something to do with the many strange incidents that had happened in the house for the past nine years. She forgot all about the pancakes and crouched down to see her daughter eye to eye.

"What does this lady look like?" she asked Debbie, trying not to let on how scared she had suddenly become.

"She's old, like Grandma," answered Debbie. "And her dress is black, like Daddy's car."

"And the boy?"

"He's three, like me," she said. "Mom, the pancakes!" she yelled and pointed above her mother's head.

Fanny stood up and took the smoking pancakes off the griddle and put them into the trash. As she started pour the batter to make more, she began to shiver at the thought of what might happen to Debbie if they kept living in this haunted house.

When Debbie asked Sam who the lady and the boy were, he just told her she had dreamt them and that there was nothing to worry about, but even he seemed to be a bit concerned by the news. Fanny and Sam kept tabs on the situation by asking her every day if she had been visited by the two strange figures and what they did on those days.

The last straw came when Debbie announced to her mother that the old lady had seen fit to spank her one night. Fanny's face turned red with anger at the news.

"It's okay, Mommy, it didn't hurt."

But Fanny's rage did not fade. After nine years in the haunted house, she decided that it was time to move.

*   *   *

Clare Walsh realized it was the first time she had ever been alone in their new house. Her husband, George, still hadn't returned from work and their two daughters, Wendy, 10, and Sandy, 20, had gone out to get some groceries she needed to finish the supper she was currently preparing. They had moved in two weeks earlier and were renting the house from its former residents, the Furrys, who they had never met since the whole rental process had been handled by a third party. Clare liked the house and the neighborhood and had suggested to George that, when they had some money saved, they put in an offer to buy the house permanently, but that was probably a few years away from happening.

From behind her the sound of a tiny whine reminded her that she wasn't completely alone in the house; it was their dog, Chester, a brown-haired mutt they had rescued from the pound years ago.

"What's the matter, Chester?" she asked, assuming he was just begging for a scrap or two. She was surprised to see him looking away from her, cowering on the kitchen floor and shivering with fear. "What is it, boy?" she kneeled down and petted him. He whined again and she looked up in the direction he was facing and dropped the wooden the spoon she had been holding.

There in the kitchen doorway she saw a white, misty haze. Even though it was not solid, she could see that it was coming together to form a human shape. She had no idea how she was supposed to react to such a strange sight and before she could find out, Chester found enough courage to get up and bark at the mist, causing it to instantly vanish.

At first she kept what happened that evening to herself, but as the months passed, she started hearing sounds like footsteps and loud banging throughout the house at different hours of the day. Clare decided it would be in her best interest to investigate the history of the house: was it really haunted or was she just losing her mind?

She got her first chance to learn about the house when she and her husband went next door to eat with their neighbors, the Kurus. As nonchalantly as she could, she asked them if they had heard any stories about strange things that had happened at the house in the past. Much to her relief both of them nodded at the same time.

"We almost bought the house," Mr. Kuru told her, "before the Furrys picked it up. But when we came to see it for a second time we ran into a fellow who lives down the street from here. He told us that he knew the selling owners and had seen several odd things in that house that had convinced him the place was haunted. He suggested we find another house to buy and, luckily for us, this one right next door to it went up for sale just a few days later."

With this news, Clare decided to contact the neighbor who had convinced the Kurus to buy another house. He turned out to be a retired gentleman who was only too happy to discuss with her why he believed the house was haunted.

"When I moved into the neighborhood in '51, people were still talking about the fellow who owned the house in the early '40s. I can never remember his name—Gumm, I think, or something close to it. He was supposed to be an odd character. Made his money in the circus, a lot of it from what I've heard, but he was one of those folks who wouldn't trust a banker as far as you could throw him—especially after the crash of '29. So instead of keeping his money in a bank, he converted it into gold coins, which he stashed in hiding spots all around his house. Trouble is that some of his hiding spots were so clever that he couldn't remember where they were, and he had never thought to make a map. He found most of these spots before he died in, I think it was '43, maybe '44. From what I heard, there was quite a lot of his money still hidden in that place that he hadn't been able to find again. My guess is that all of that strange stuff that happens in that house happens because Gumm, or whatever his name was, wants to find the rest of his money."

Clare found herself becoming more and more excited as she listened to the old man talk. By the time he was finished she had almost forgotten about the ghost in her house and was instead focusing on the idea that it might contain hidden stashes of lost treasure. The first thing she did when she got home was write up a list of anything even slightly amiss in the house that might prove that the story was true. Among the items on the list was the fact that the attic door refused to close properly, as if something was keeping it from shutting tight. Deciding to investigate it first, she went to the door and opened it. She noticed that the first step to the attic was slightly askew and was the reason the door couldn't be closed. She bent over to check it out and discovered that the top of the step lifted away in her hand, revealing a small empty hiding space. Though she was disappointed not to find any gold coins, she at least now had evidence that the story was true.

Now that she knew where one of the former owner's hiding spots was, she paid careful attention to that area. One night, she heard the attic door open and close four times. She got up to investigate and saw that everyone else in the house was asleep. She found that the attic door, which had been closed when she went to bed, was now open. She shut it and went back to sleep, only to find it wide open again when she got up in the morning.

Then she began to notice the sound of footsteps going up and down the attic stairs. After a few weeks of hearing these phantom footfalls, she noticed that they always seemed to pause near the spot where she had found the empty hiding space. It was as if the spirit responsible for making the sound was stopping to make sure all of the coins were taken out of that particular stash.

She was truly convinced that the old man's theory was correct when she went to retrieve an item she needed from the attic and found many of the boxes and items had been moved since the last time she was in there, just a few hours earlier. Most of the stuff had been moved so someone could get to the old chest of drawers near the back of the space. Before it would have been impossible to open any of these drawers, but now she could see that one of them was no longer fully closed. She stepped over the boxes in her way to get to the old chest. Inside the open drawer was a series of blueprints of the house with several spots circled, including where she had found the hiding space in the attic stairway. There, at the bottom of each blueprint, was a name. It turned out that old man had been wrong about one thing. The ghost's name wasn't Gumm, it was Gehm. Henry Gehm.

At last Clare thought she had answered the question of just who was responsible for haunting her family's home, when her daughter Wendy told her that she had seen the ghost of a little boy in her room—the same room that had once belonged to Debbie Furry. But unlike Debbie, Wendy was never visited by the woman in the black dress. She did, however, witness several other unexplainable occurrences. One night she was awoken by the sound of her typewriter whirring and clicking as if the world's fastest typist was at its keys. She got up just in time to see the keys move up and down on their own accord, and suddenly stop. Clare wondered if the spirit responsible for this sudden burst of furious writing was trying to send the family a message. If it was, its efforts were wasted since

Clare found many of the boxes and items had moved since the last time she was in there.

there hadn't been any paper in the typewriter and its words went unrecorded.

Eventually the number of paranormal events in the house grew so numerous that the Walshes found themselves becoming inured to them. Clare and George got so used to finding the contents of their drawers in disarray—as if someone had been searching through them—that they eventually stopped reorganizing them. They no longer commented on lights that had turned on by themselves and instead just turned them off without a word. They ceased to notice the sounds of the footsteps and ignored the muffled cries that could occasionally be heard coming from within the house's walls. They got so used to it all that they might have stayed in the house, were it not for the effect the haunting was having on their furriest member.

Since the first time he and Clare had seen the ghostly presence in the kitchen, Chester, the Walshes' dog, had long ceased to be the happy-go-lucky pooch they remembered. Where once his whole life had been an extremely satisfying hodge-podge of naps, games of fetch, barking at insects and cats, naps, belly rubs and begging for treats, he was now just a frightened shell of his former self. He barely had the will to nap, let alone any other beloved former activities. So for the sake of Chester, the Walshes decided to move. And to ensure that they didn't have to deal with this same problem again, they decided to build a new house rather than face dealing with an older house's haunted history ever again.

*   *   *

Robert and June Wheeler were the next couple to move into the house and—like the Furrys and the Walshes before them—they quickly caught wind of its paranormal peculiarities. But unlike the house's previous tenants, the Wheelers decided to go beyond a cursory investigation into their new home's history and really find out everything they could about Henry Gehm and his former home.

They found out that Gehm had made his fortune manufacturing railway cars and not in the circus as had been previously reported (though he had leased several of his cars to different circuses from that period, which explains how this mistake could have been made). Gehm was suspicious enough of banks to ferret away his savings in various nooks and crannies of his house. They also found out that—despite previous assertions to the contrary—Gehm had recovered all of his hidden loot before his death, much to the chagrin of treasure hunters who, to this day, come to the famous haunted house in hopes of finding long-lost gold coins.

Still, despite the inaccuracies in the house's legend, the Wheelers are certain that Gehm haunts their home, along with a host of other spirits they have yet to identify. They believe that the young boy who visited both the Furrys' and Walshes' young daughters is most likely the ghost of Gehm's six-year-old grandson, who died while the eccentric railway entrepreneur lived in the house. And despite the presence of so many unaccountable spirits, they have grown comfortable in their haunted home.

In the past 50 years the unassuming house in the St. Louis neighborhood of Webster Grove has become one of the most famous haunted houses in North America. As three different families have moved in and out of the famous abode, each has been forced to decide whether or not to accept the house's many strange quirks and novelties. In the long run, two of those families could not handle the strain of owning a haunted home, but eventually the Gehm House fell into the hands of a couple who not only could handle that strain, but also embraced it as one of the house's virtues. To some, their willingness to live among these spirits might not make any sense, but in a world where good anecdotes are so hard to find, their choice to live in a place that has elicited so many interesting stories seems perfectly sensible.

Betty Ruth

"Granny?" Betty Ruth Ward shouted through her grand-mother's back door. "Are you home?"

"I'm in here, honey," answered a voice from the living room.

That was confirmation enough for the energetic nine-year-old to come inside the house and run to the living room, where she found her Granny shelling a large bowl of walnuts.

"Watcha doin'?" she asked playfully, even though she knew the answer.

"Jasper Redfern gave me a big bag of walnuts for help-ing him cure that nasty patch of fungus that was growing on the bottom of his foot."

"Ewwww, that's yucky, Granny." Betty Ruth scrunched up her face.

"There's nothing yucky about it, honey. It just doesn't feel so good when you got it."

"Why are you shelling them all?"

"I'm going to do some baking. There's a church fundraiser coming up and I thought I could sell my wal-nut brownies to help raise some money."

"Can I help?"

"Sure you can, as long as you don't make too much of a mess."

"I won't," Betty Ruth promised, even though she doubted she'd be able to keep that promise. She had a tal-ent for making messes and there had yet to be a situation she faced where she hadn't been able to show it.

That's not to say that she was deliberately destructive. She had never in her life set out to make a mess; it just seemed to happen somehow, as if some strange force was determined to keep her in a constant state of trouble. She tried explaining this to her parents, but they refused to believe her, choosing instead to insist that her many "accidents" were the result of her fidgety, excitable nature. For this reason she did her very best to shell the walnuts as neatly as she possibly could. Her grandmother noticed her effort and complimented her.

"You're a real natural with that nutcracker," she said as she smiled at her granddaughter.

"Thanks, Granny." Betty Ruth blushed, grateful for the praise.

"Would you like some lemonade?"

"Yes, please," she answered with a smile.

As her grandmother went to the kitchen to make a pitcher of lemonade, Betty Ruth continued to shell the walnuts in front of her as tidily as she could. Now alone in the living room she started humming a tune she had learned last week at Sunday school. The humming put her in the mood to listen to some music, so she put down her nutcracker, got up and ran into the kitchen.

"Granny, can I turn on the radio?"

"As long as you don't turn it to that rolling and rocking station," she answered. "You know I don't approve of that hip-swinging music."

"Awww, Granny!" protested Betty Ruth. She was a big fan of Elvis Presley.

"Don't you aw me, young lady. My house, my rules."

"Ooo-kay." Betty Ruth sulked as she walked back into the living room. She turned on the radio and kept it on the station it was already on. The sound of country music filled the room. Betty Ruth liked the way the fiddle sounded, so she didn't mind that it wasn't Elvis she was listening to.

She went back to the table and started shelling more walnuts as she moved in her chair in time to the music. Distracted by the tune, her nutcracking skills became somewhat diminished, but she was still managing to avoid making too much of a mess until she glanced up at the bowl of shelled walnuts and saw something very odd.

The walnuts were *dancing* in time with the music.

Betty Ruth's mouth dropped open at the sight of this bizarre occurrence, but before she could call out to her grandmother, the dancing walnuts started jumping out of their bowl. Some flew out to the nearby curtains, which they started to climb. Others floated in mid-air, as if they were suspended by invisible strings, while the rest jumped all the way up to the ceiling. Then, just seconds after this had all started, the song ended and they all tumbled down to the ground, evidently unwilling to continue boogying to the sound of a toothpaste commercial.

"Betty Ruth!" her grandmother yelled when she saw the mess that surrounded the young girl. Both shelled and unshelled walnuts lay everywhere around the living room. She shook her head with disbelief as she set down the tray she was carrying. "I leave you alone for five minutes. Do you realize how long it is going to take us to clean this up?"

"But I didn't do it!" protested Betty Ruth.

"Stop! I have no patience for any of your lies."

Not your average walnut.

"But I swear I didn't! The nuts just started dancing on their own. They flew out of the bowl all by themselves. I had nothing to do with it, honest!"

"Do I look like a fool, Betty Ruth Ward? Because only a fool would believe a story as ridiculous as that!"

Before Betty Ruth could insist that she did not think her grandmother was a fool, the commercial on the radio ended and another song began. At once the walnuts jumped back into the air, just as they had just a minute before. Betty Ruth's grandmother was so shocked to see it with her own eyes that she screamed aloud.

"I told you!" Betty Ruth said triumphantly, before her grandmother grabbed her by her arm and started dragging her out of the house. "But I want to watch," she said as her grandmother pushed her through the front door. She lost the battle to remain inside and followed her grandmother as she ran to the family farm down the road.

Betty Ruth's parents were sitting in the kitchen, listening to the radio, when she and her grandmother burst breathlessly through the backdoor. Her grandmother was so winded she couldn't speak as she collapsed into the closest chair.

"The walnuts were floating!" Betty Ruth explained to her shocked parents. "Really! They were!"

"What are you going on about?" asked her father.

"They floated right out of the bowl and danced to the music on the radio!"

He turned and asked his mother, who was just starting to catch her breath, "Mama, what is she talking about?"

"It's true...I saw them," she said between gasps for air. "The walnuts were...floating."

Betty Ruth's mother frowned. "Mama Ward, have you been nipping at Jasper Redfern's 'shine again?"

"No," she answered, obviously offended that her daughter-in-law could have even suggested such a thing.

"Are you sure, Mama?" asked her son. "Do you remember the last time you drank a shot of that stuff? You said you saw a flying saucer up in the sky."

"You never mind what I said I saw last time, Clinton Ward." She defended herself, having caught her second wind. "I tell you I just saw—"

Before she could continue, the bowl of fruit on the table in front of them began to shudder and shake.

"See!" Betty Ruth pointed as the bowl lifted itself off the table and floated in mid-air.

A pair of coffee cups, a potted plant and several assorted knick-knacks that Mrs. Ward had used to decorate her kitchen soon joined the bowl of fruit as they floated in ways none of those objects should have been logically capable of floating.

The adults were too stunned to react, but Betty Ruth heard the sound of the radio and ran over to it and turned it off. The music stopped and the laws of gravity once more came into effect, causing all of the floating objects to crash back down to the spots they had been originally occupying.

"Well," Betty Ruth's father said as he scratched the back of his head, "wasn't that something?"

It sure was.

*　　*　　*

Not knowing what else to do, Mr. Ward called the sheriff, who—upon hearing what had happened—contacted a friend of his who knew something about ghosts. This friend in turn contacted William Cox and

Jim Bethel, two professional paranormal researchers employed by Duke University's Parapsychology Laboratory. They were intrigued by the Ward's story and decided to visit the farm in Hartville to investigate the situation for themselves.

For the first few hours nothing happened, but that all changed when Betty Ruth came home from school. Almost immediately the two researchers were inundated with a series of incredible occurrences. They saw a can of shoe polish float in the air, followed by a bar of soap and then a pot of stew. In each instance the levitating objects came down with a crash, causing some kind of mess. The black shoe polish splattered all over the floor, the bar of soap exploded into a thousand tiny fragments and the stew ended up decorating the kitchen wall.

They followed Betty Ruth as she went outside to play and for their effort they were rewarded by being pelted with rocks, pieces of bark and even a few stray walnuts before they retreated back into the safety of inside. The evidence led them inexorably to one firm conclusion. The Wards had a poltergeist on their hands and—for some reason they could not explain—this destructive spirit was fixated on their young daughter.

Betty Ruth's history of destruction suddenly made sense. Messes didn't suddenly happen around her because she was careless or clumsy, but because she was being followed by a special kind of ghost who specialized in creating chaos. Her parents felt incredibly guilty for all of the times they punished her for breaking something, even when she proclaimed her innocence. She had been telling them the truth all along—well, at least most of the time.

How all this happened or where the spirit had come from was impossible to determine. Poltergeists, unlike most other spirits, tend not to leave any clues as to their identities, choosing instead to simply remain nameless, faceless, destructive forces. The researchers told the Wards that there was no way to determine just how long these cases of phantom mayhem would take place. Some poltergeists attack specific spots just once and only for a few minutes, while others remain for decades before their mischief finally ceases. The spirit that followed Betty Ruth could be with her for just a few more days or for the rest of her life; there was simply no way to know for sure.

Just before Cox and Bethel left the farm, they witnessed another example of the spirit's destructive streak when a large washtub full of laundry flew off the farmhouse's front porch and crashed down with a muddy splash to the ground just in front of Betty Ruth's feet.

*   *   *

As Betty Ruth got older, the number of strange incidents on the farm began to decrease. She was a smart little girl and had long ago learned how to turn her strange situation to her advantage. Now she was free to be as careless and clumsy as she pleased, knowing that the ghost that followed her would inevitably get the blame. By the time she reached her teens, she was the only person who had any way of knowing when something genuinely paranormal had occurred on the farm, but sometimes even she couldn't tell herself. As she grew older and less prone to mischief, the accidents became less frequent until they gradually stopped altogether. The truth was that the poltergeist could have left years before then, but there was simply no way to know for sure beyond asking Betty Ruth.

And she wasn't telling.

The End

LONE
PINE

Lone Pine Publishing International

If you enjoyed this book, you'll want to
read these fascinating accounts of
paranormal folklore throughout the South.

NEW MAY 2006
Ghost Stories of Georgia *by Chris Wangler*

From the hustle and bustle of Atlanta to the haunted squares of Savannah and beyond, *Ghost Stories of Georgia* will frighten, amaze and entertain you. Read about Sir Godfrey Barnsley, a model for Rhett Butler in *Gone with the Wind*, who is forced to confront the terrifying power of a Cherokee curse at his lavish mansion in Adairsville. Discover a tale of forbidden love lurking behind a haunting at the Midway Cemetery. Meet a melancholy ghost called Mary the Wanderer, who materializes on St. Simons Island with her guiding lamp.

$11.95USD/$14.95CDN • ISBN10:1-894877-74-8 • ISBN13: 978-1-894877-74-9 • 5.25" x 8.25" • 240 pages

NEW AUGUST 2006
Ghost Stories of Virginia *by Dan Asfar*

The hanged pirates of Blackbeard are among the restless spirits who make up this collection of folklore from the historic state of Virginia. It is said you can hear the pirates moaning and the sounds of gallows creaking along the Williamsburg road where they were hanged. In Midlothian, a former plantation house nearly as old as Virginia itself, a preacher banishes the ghosts of two star-crossed lovers into the bottom of a well, which remains sealed to this very day. Read these tales and many more.

$11.95USD/$14.95CDN • ISBN10:976-8200-19-7 • ISBN13:978-976-8200-19-8 • 5.25" x 8.25" • 224 pages

Ghost Stories of the Old South *by Edrick Thay*

Tales of the unexplained and of inevitable tragedy are part of the folklore that makes the Old South one of America's most storied regions. Discover centers of paranormal lore, such as Savannah, Charleston and Raleigh, or learn about stubborn yet genteel ghosts obsessed with the survival of Old Dixie.

$10.95USD/$14.95CDN • ISBN10: -894877-18-7 • ISBN13:978-1-894877-18-3 • 5.25" x 8.25" • 200 pages

Ghost Stories of the Civil War *by Dan Asfar and Edrick Thay*

The four years of the U.S Civil War claimed the lives of 600,000 Americans and left much of the country in ruins. This collection features many stories about restless spirits for whom the war is not yet over. Eyewitnesses swear they've seen the ghosts of Abraham Lincoln, Jefferson Davis and Edgar Allan Poe at Fort Monroe, one of the few Union forts in the Confederate South. "Old Green Eyes," the disembodied head of a fallen soldier, terrifies visitors to Chickamauga and Chattanooga National Military Park in Georgia. In the cemetery of a former Ohio war prison, a battalion of Confederate dead rise from their anonymous graves. These stories and many more will keep you up half the night!

$10.95USD/$14.95CDN • ISBN10:1-894877-16-0 • ISBN13:978-1-894877-16-9 • 5.25" x 8.25" • 216 pages

These and many more LPPI books are available
from your local bookseller or by ordering direct.
U.S. readers call 1-800-518-3541. In Canada, call 1-800-661-9017.